THE STARTER GUIDE TO RAISING BACKYARD CHICKENS

7 STEPS TO A HAPPY FLOCK, HEALTHY EGGS, AND BECOMING SELF-SUFFICIENT

MACOMB FARMS

CONTENTS

A SPECIAL GIFT TO OUR READERS

Included with your purchase of this book is Chicken Health 101: Chicken Keeper Beginner Basics. This resource contains the prevention method, health checklist, first aid kit supplies, common sicknesses and diseases, and the healthy chicken diet.

Scan the QR code below and let us know which email to deliver it to:

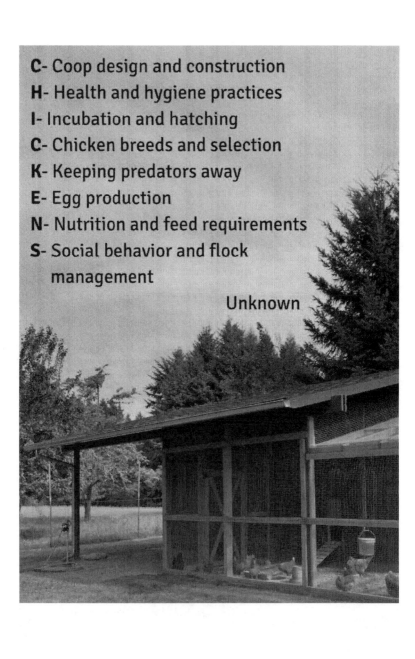

C- Coop design and construction
H- Health and hygiene practices
I- Incubation and hatching
C- Chicken breeds and selection
K- Keeping predators away
E- Egg production
N- Nutrition and feed requirements
S- Social behavior and flock
   management

Unknown

INTRODUCTION

Let me set the dream scenario for you. You wake up to the sound of chickens clucking outside your bedroom window. You walk out into the fresh morning air and greet your dozen feathered friends. When you open the gate to their coop, they run out, excited to eat kernels of corn from your hand. As the chickens peck at their feed in your yard, you enter the coop and retrieve a dozen crisp, warm eggs, ready to hit the frying pan. You enjoy your fresh-from-the-farm breakfast and overlook your vibrant, natural garden with a satisfied sigh.

The kind of pride you achieve knowing that you can provide healthy, organic food for yourself and your family: This is the confidence of self-sufficiency. This book will help you imagine how it feels to have these birds in your backyard, experience the all-encompassing pleasure of working with nature, and benefit from your labor like many have and will.

Let your imagination run wild as I take you through the seven steps to a happy flock, healthy eggs, and becoming self-sufficient. Raising chickens helps you rest peacefully, knowing you are doing right by your family and the environment. Watching these barnyard birds go about their business is soothing, relaxing, and entertaining. Chicken rearing can be therapeutic, gratifying, and pleasant. They help fill your family's life with memories of working with nature and its natural cycles. They ask for so little and give so much. Chickens are well-known among poultry growers for their distinct personalities and quirkiness. They're known for their "funny antics" (Kelly, 2012) and, more importantly, for being as emotionally supportive as any dog, cat, bird, or other pet.

Why raise chickens? It's a valid question, but if you enjoy eggs or chicken meat and have the space, you'd be crazy not to keep your own flock. Raising chickens assists you in becoming self-sufficient, meaning you'll never need to buy eggs from a store once you have hens. Many people have a keen idea of what raising chickens look like but are initially uncertain of where to begin. Thinking about everything necessary to keep chickens can feel overwhelming.

Because people aren't born knowing how to care for chickens, it's okay not to know everything there is to know about them. It can be challenging to determine what information to believe from the numerous resources available today. Having all the information you need in one accessible location can save you hundreds of hours attempting to conduct your research. This book covers all you need to know about keeping chickens for eggs and comprehensively introduces different chicken breeds, housing, feeding, health, and all you need to know about egg production.

If you are...

- unsure where to start when keeping backyard hens
- tired of the rat race and want to live a more peaceful and harmonious life closer to nature
- someone interested in self-sufficient living with a chicken flock
- afraid of ingesting artificial chemicals and preservatives from retail goods such as eggs

...then you've landed at the right place. This book will help you to realize a part of your vision of living closer to nature by raising backyard chickens.

What will you learn in this book?

- I will show you how to ensure that your chickens produce high-quality eggs.
- You'll discover how to live a healthy, artificial-free life that's connected to nature and sustainable.
- We'll review any health or maintenance issues, so you don't have to deal with the consequences of an under-maintained brood.
- You will learn how to deal with predators. Nothing is more upsetting than discovering that an animal has broken into your coop or yard and slaughtered your chickens.
- We will explore diseases, parasites, and other concerns all chicken owners face. Mites, lice, and other bugs can overwhelm your flock, or an invasive rodent can bring unwanted pests with them.
- I will show you that it's okay to take vacations or long weekends and leave your chickens unattended for that time. That you can't is nothing more than a lie.
- Finally, you will learn about one of the most significant challenges—feed costs—which we have little influence over. Those trying to

consume a certified organic or GMO-free diet may face even more financial challenges.

I suggest not purchasing chickens to save money at the grocery store. If you value self-sufficiency, like seeing and being around chickens, and want super-fresh, super-healthy eggs, then take the plunge and get yourself a flock. These factors have significantly more impact on your life than merely saving money.

You must agree to specific terms when you wish to adopt an animal. These responsibilities include feeding and caring for them; we all want the best for our loved ones. Our creatures are entitled to nothing less and will become part of the family like any other animal.

People have not always kept animals solely to have a pet; animals have only been held for companionship over the last hundred years. Before this, practically everyone had animals for work, whether meat, eggs, milk, or to help with hunting or pest management. Companionship is a bonus of having such a friendly animal. It's no surprise that you and many others are increasingly interested in rearing a flock of chickens because this is built into us as humans.

As an animal lover who enjoys getting something extra from their care, I wrote this book to explain everything you need to know about raising chickens so you can reap the same benefits. I want to share my expertise and experience to help you benefit from your flock. I'll show you how to grow and care for chickens to get the most out of them.

I want to assist you in this venture by teaching you and alleviating any anxiety about taking care of delicate young chicks; you don't want to be the source of any suffering or trouble. I will help relieve any concerns about selecting healthy stock and ensuring that they produce enough high-quality eggs, as this may be one of the main reasons you want to raise chickens. I will provide the necessary information about what you should give them at each stage of their development to ensure they receive the finest nutrition possible.

I address all these issues in this book and others. I will dispel your doubts about the subject, motivate you to start growing your flock, and provide you with the knowledge you need to succeed. Many people feel that rearing birds is an expensive and time-consuming endeavor. When you consider the cost of raising and keeping birds compared to the eggs or meat you will receive, you will realize that it is relatively inexpensive. You will soon have a continuous supply of high-quality meat and eggs as well as the satisfaction of watching these lovely creatures grow while raising them. So be ready to learn everything you need to start your own backyard flock.

1

WHY RAISE CHICKENS?

W hen it comes to chickens, you must be practical. You should be sure that this commitment is appropriate for you; animals are not disposable items that can be discarded if you no longer want them. Rehoming birds is more complicated than rehoming other pets, so be sure you're ready for the commitment before you start.

Living with hens is eye-opening because they are not the foolish birds frequently depicted. They have excellent memories, are intelligent, can learn tricks, have their own language, and recognize over a hundred different chickens and people.

In this chapter, you'll learn the many advantages of owning hens and some downsides before diving into all the information you should consider before embarking on your chicken-keeping adventure.

✚ THE BENEFITS OF RAISING CHICKENS

High-Quality Eggs

Chickens that spend the entire day as your pets—roaming freely, eating quality feed, and living stress-free—regularly lay fresh, tasty, and nutrient-dense eggs. You and your family will enjoy the best chicken eggs available.

Breakfast has firmly established itself as the most important meal of the day, thanks to the excellent eggs produced by chickens. Freshly laid eggs are significantly superior to those from factory hens. Free-range eggs from backyard chickens are much richer in nutritional value. They have been shown to contain seven times the amount of vitamin A and double the amount of vitamin E, on top of much more significant amounts of omega-3s and beta carotene and lower saturated fat.

With chickens in your backyard, you will not have to worry about buying eggs because you can walk out to the coop in your pajamas and come back with supplies for breakfast. You don't have to worry about the variety of confusing egg labels in the stores like non-cage-free, cage-free, and organic. Understanding how mass-produced eggs are handled and labeled and precisely what those egg packaging codes imply is the key to confidently purchasing a carton of eggs (Freeman, 2022).

Furthermore, you have complete control over what gets into your eggs. Hens are given high-quality feed rich in vitamins A and E, which guarantees that they produce eggs with the same vitamins, but they prefer table leftovers, bugs, and weeds. This diet will provide you with the best eggs you've ever tasted.

Depending on your daily egg needs, you may have too many eggs to eat. Chickens usually lay one egg daily, but some lay three to four weekly. These eggs can be sold at farmer's markets or to friends, neighbors, and local restaurants, among other places. Because free-range, organic, local eggs are a specialty worldwide, you should be able to sell these eggs for a reasonable price. If willing, you can have your children sell the eggs as an entrepreneurship activity.

Self-Sufficiency

Raising hens may appear to be a complex undertaking at first, but as you gain experience, your confidence will grow. Achieving a new skill, self-sufficiency, is part of this boost in confidence. Raising chickens allows you to generate and grow your own food. In an industrialized world, impersonal farming, and agricultural practices such as battery farming and factory farming are the norm.

You will not only be self-sufficient, but you will also be able to live in harmony with nature. You will be adding to nature rather than taking from it if you learn how to care for animals. You will experience the pleasure of seeing another living being flourish due to your efforts. You will form bonds with these birds, and they will form bonds with you.

Kills Bugs, Weeds, and Pests

Bugs and weeds are the choice feed for chickens. Because the chickens will keep your house, yard, and garden clean and pristine, this is ideal. You won't need pesticides or insecticides since your chickens will spend the entire day looking for grasshoppers, snails, slugs, ladybugs, and other creepy crawlies. If some fruit falls to the ground, don't worry; your pet will eat it before it attracts bugs and other pests. These multi-tasking birds also serve as vacuum cleaners for leftovers, eager to consume all crumbs and remains from your regular meals. Vegetable peels, fruits, seeds, nuts, and other waste are chickens' favorites. Allowing them to feed as much as they want on the scraps will produce some tasty eggs.

Chickens will not only get rid of weeds in your yard, but they will also get rid of mice, small snakes, and other pests. A snake may slither onto your land in search of chicken eggs. It will be met by a full-grown chicken, a bit large for a snake to swallow. Because chickens are flock animals, if one chicken tries to kill a snake, the others will swarm to the snake to assist in killing it. Although a hen may kill a snake with a few swipes of her beak, its swift and sharp strikes will usually leave a snake unrecognizable.

Excellent Fertilizers

Chicken manure is one of the most productive animal manures available. Chicken dung, when adequately composted, releases potassium, nitrogen, and phosphorus into your soil. However, do not use fresh chicken manure in your garden. I usually wait a month for the waste to degrade before adding it to my compost pile. In addition, I compost all the dry leaves and shavings from my coop. If you wish to use chicken dung, ensure your chickens have access to an enclosure with bedding where they can sleep every night. If you let them go free, they will relieve themselves anywhere they please, making it difficult to collect their dung once a month.

Delicious Meat

One of the best aspects of keeping a chicken is that you may acquire a taste for fresh, free-range, organic fried chicken now and then. Homegrown chicken is healthier since it has fewer calories, fat, hormones, and pesticides. Most importantly, it tastes better.

You may be unable to slaughter your pets because you have become too attached to them. If this is the case, it's no doubt better not to build bonds with your hens if you plan to consume them later.

Weeding

We leave our chickens to free range, which allows them to have an excellent quality of life, ranging wherever they choose, and they help keep the garden looking lovely and free of weeds. To keep predators away from the chickens, we ensure the backyard is well-secured with chicken wire fences.

Pleasure

Like people, chickens have unique personalities and quirks, which makes raising them so enjoyable and entertaining. Chicken owners love their time watching "chicken tv" and learning each chicken's characteristics. Ours regularly walk inside the house or leap on the windowsills because they are free-range. They've been known to enter the greenhouse, as well. Chickens enjoy exploring, playing, and scratching around for bugs and seeds.

Family Amusement

Taking care of chickens is a fun family pastime and can create great memories. It can be an excellent way to teach youngsters about responsibilities, tasks, animal care, the significance of cleaning animal enclosures, collecting eggs, and securing the grounds where the chickens are housed, among other things.

Cuts Down on Kitchen Waste

Chickens eat different foods and will gladly consume typical kitchen waste such as leftover bread crusts, vegetable peelings, or oatmeal. They'll eat soft fruit, nuts, and spoiled seeds.

Be a Part of a Community

Many people have tiny plots of land or perform some farming in their backyards. It's a terrific way to connect with others who share your interests, whether they're neighbors, coworkers, or people you meet online. This will revitalize your activities, and there will be plenty of individuals to offer advice if you run into problems.

Low-Cost and Low Maintenance

Raising chickens can be inexpensive or costly, depending on your motivations and strategy. Chicks can be purchased for a small price. Baby chicks, for example, may be purchased for $6 each. Installing a chicken coop is simple and basic; most coops come pre-assembled and cost less than $200. Similarly, chicken feeding is cost-effective because they offer regular nourishment and can generate cash through eggs, chicks, or meat. Chickens are excellent pets for anyone on a budget because they are inexpensive, easy to care for, and don't require much attention. When caring for chickens, you don't need acres of land. A small or medium backyard is plenty big enough for a couple of chickens to run around.

Lucrative

Chicken care is generally inexpensive because hens do not require much equipment or care to survive. Chickens do fine if they are kept in a coop with enough shade, food, and water. You can start a poultry farm if you prefer. Broiler hens, for example, mature after a few months. You can keep some of the first batch's eggs to hatch, sell the remainder for profit, and start the procedure over again. Breeding free-range hens provides a fair return on your initial investment.

Mental Wellness

You can quickly find yourself relating to your chickens. Most studies come to the same conclusion: Our pets improve our physical and emotional well-being. Pet care can lower blood pressure, calm your heart rate, reduce stress, and stress hormones (such as cortisol), boost self-esteem and well-being, and make us feel loved (Newport Academy, 2021). Your breathing becomes more regular and muscle tension reduces when you stroke or snuggle a pet. We now have animal-assisted therapy programs because animals are so good for mental health. Your new pets could be a great way to boost your mental health and make you healthier and happier.

THE DOWNSIDES OF RAISING CHICKENS

Initial Investment

While your chicks will be inexpensive (typically under $8 per bird), you need a coop and some accessories. You will save a lot of money if you can modify a shed or outbuilding to their needs. The enclosure is frequently the most expensive component of the setup. Remember that most predators eat hens, so your coop should give predation protection and a dry, draft-free living place. Most other items you'll need, such as feeders and waterers, are inexpensive and can be found at a feed store or online.

The Poop!

Aside from laying eggs, chickens are also excellent at pooping. An average hen is believed to dump roughly 130 pounds of manure yearly, which is a lot of poop! Let's do some math: 130 times 12 birds, for example, would be 1,560 pounds. You'll have to clean up all this waste and dispose of it somewhere. You can use old manure on your garden bed if you have one. You can sprinkle manure to fertilize the soil if no plants are growing in the beds. It's an excellent fertilizer, but you can't apply it directly to your plants since it'll burn and destroy them instead of enriching them. However, in the winter, this restriction no longer applies.

Death and Illness

Chickens can get sick. It can be challenging to detect illnesses because they hide disease as a survival technique. Finding a trained, local veterinarian can be tricky, so you must educate yourself or join a knowledgeable group to find the proper treatment for any illness among your chickens. Death can strike without notice and without a specific cause. This can be devastating to a new chicken keeper but know it does sometimes happen just out of the blue, and you could not have done anything differently to prevent it.

The Laying of Eggs Will End

After the first 18 months, hens will slow down in output. They will continue to lay eggs, although not as frequently as before. It would be best if you decide ahead of time what you will do with them once they have ceased to be productive. Will you let them live out their natural lives (they can live for 8–10 years), or will you cull them for a meal?

Gorgeous Gardens

Keep your chicken out of your garden if you enjoy growing beautiful flowers and fresh food. Chickens can be helpful in the yard, but they enjoy digging, scratching, and dust bathing, which will devastate your plants and flowers. You can open up the spaces for your hens in the fall once your vegetables and flowers are dead. Picking bugs, poking around for weed seeds, and tasting any falling fruits will be a blast. Chickens are excellent soil cultivators and pest control agents.

Feeding

If you want organic chickens, you can feed them leftover food and scraps from the kitchen if you eat a balanced diet. Bread, corn, grains, oats, fruits, and raw vegetables are favorites of birds.

Raw potato peels, salt, damaged or rotten foods, coffee or coffee grounds, citrus fruits, soft drinks, chocolate, oily foods, and processed foods are all hazardous to chickens. You should not feed your chickens garlic, onions, or other strong-tasting items since they alter their eggs' flavor.

You'll still have to feed your chickens organic chick starter, crumbles, and layer pellets (though the layer pellets come later). Grit, a mixture of small rocks that helps chickens digest their food, is also necessary. Every day, allow your chickens to run around in the backyard. Because they eat the stones in the yard, they don't require as much store-bought grit. Organic chicken feed is abundant in protein, which helps your birds lay great eggs and keeps their feathers healthy. This may cost you around $30 per month for 5 chickens, which you could recoup by selling eggs.

On the other hand, your chickens can live for another 8 years after they stop laying eggs, costing you money and time without the added advantage of laying eggs. Hens become more challenging to prepare and consume as they age. For example, if you have eight chickens, you will have to spend money and time caring for them for several years after they stop providing eggs. To keep them healthy, you'll need to give them scraps, vegetable peelings, supplements, seeds, etc. In the long run, this will be costly. Furthermore, you may want to purchase younger hens to produce more eggs, which will cost you even more money.

You will be wasting a lot of time, money, and effort on a chicken that no longer produces food and may be too old to be sold for meat if you cannot part with her after this period because you have bonded with her. You must be willing to spend money on your hens as pets who only give you friendship, camaraderie, and loyalty.

Chickens Can Be Mean

The story of mean hens holds some truth. Chickens can be loyal and kind pets, but they can also be vicious bullies. They've been known to peck each other till they bleed, even killing a helpless chicken. However, because chickens are gregarious animals, they cannot be kept alone and have been known to die of loneliness.

State Regulations

You'll need to investigate the laws in your area regarding owning hens. Ordinances at your local city hall or zoning office will specify how many birds you can keep, how much land you can keep them on, and how close to highways and buildings they can be. Regulations also specify whether you require a permit and whether you must register, apply for planning approval, and have your coop inspected. Furthermore, an ordinance will inform you whether keeping a rooster is permissible.

Don't give up if your local government forbids you from raising backyard hens. You can often amend the legislation by filling out paperwork and attending local government meetings. Working with other poultry enthusiasts in the region who want to see the law modified will increase your chances of success. You can use the internet to quickly locate poultry enthusiasts in your area to join forces with. Once you have permission, notify your neighbors of your plans. Assure them that you will maintain a healthy, clean flock and make every effort to keep your hens quiet. To encourage your neighbor's trust and approval, you might offer to provide wonderful free-range eggs.

Predators

Your chicken is not just a possible food source for you but also for wild animals in the vicinity. You must bring your hens in every night if you live near predators such as foxes, possums, coyotes, skunks, weasels, or raccoons. Once predators discover your flock, keeping all of your hens safe will become difficult. Furthermore, daylight predators such as cats and dogs may also threaten your hens. Keep an eye out for hawks, eagles, and foxes. Raising backyard chickens may not be the best option if you live in a region with many predators.

If you still wish to raise chickens despite the threat of predators, you'll need to build a secure enclosure for them during the day. You may also enlist the services of a devoted companion, such as a dog, to protect your chickens.

2

GETTING READY FOR YOUR FLOCK

Now that you know the benefits and downsides of raising chickens, you might be compelled to start immediately. However, appealing the advantages sound, creating a poultry flock may not be wise, depending on your circumstances. You'll need to do some research to see if the requirements are something you can handle. You need to know if keeping hens is right for you before you start building a coop.

When starting a flock, you must consider the space needs, time requirements, and local rules governing poultry farming. Taking the time to learn about these requirements will assist you in determining whether poultry farming is suited for you at this point in your life and your current location.

CAN I RAISE CHICKENS IN MY AREA?

It can be challenging to determine whether you are permitted to keep hens in your area. However, doing homework before purchasing hens so you don't have to rehome them is worth it. A friend of mine bought hens because of her large backyard and was told she needed to rehome them due to zoning restrictions. The chickens were relocated to a lovely country house where they are well cared for, but she was disappointed.

Having chickens is not limited to those who live in rural areas. More and more individuals keep hens in their backyards in both rural and urban locations. However, you should conduct extensive research and investigation to ensure that you will not encounter any problems.

There are various places where you may look up the legislation to see if keeping chickens is legal in your area. City and county governments have laws for your protection and the well-being of the animals. The following is a list of recommended locations to look at:

Zoning Regulations in the County

Check with your local health and zoning board, planning board, county clerk, or animal control official to determine if some rules or regulations prevent raising hens in your area. You can usually find accurate contact information on your city's website.

The essential rules at the county level are the zoning laws. Some zoning restrictions limit how many animals you can keep per acre.

Covenants or Homeowners Association

Check with your neighborhood's Homeowners Association if one exists. Check your house deeds for covenants, which are regulations you must obey from the property deed and banned behaviors that may adversely influence the neighborhood.

City Code / Municipal Code

Some communities may have an online "municipal code." Also frequently referred to as a "city code." Contact any municipal authorities who have jurisdiction over your property.

Livestock Regulations

Look up "livestock ordinance" in your area on the internet. Check for specific livestock regulations as well.

Asking Questions

Make sure you ask the right questions, as certain regions may restrict the size of your flock, the facilities you keep them in, and the amount of space (acreage) required per animal. Here are some questions to consider:

- How many birds are you allowed to keep legally? Some city ordinances may only allow two or three, while others may allow 10 or more. You must provide enough space for your chickens and keep their living quarters clean and sanitary. A chicken coop should typically include 3 square feet of indoor space as well as 15 square feet of outside area per chicken. If you have additional room, that's fantastic. Disease and feather-picking are less likely to occur when hens have more significant space. Chickens require space to expand their wings, dust bathe, and bask in the sunlight.
- Can you have both hens and roosters or only hens? Roosters are frequently forbidden from being held within city borders due to their crowing, which is acceptable in the country but annoying to city dwellers. The legislation may apply to noise disturbances or nuisance animals.

- Do you have to follow any specific instructions for building the coop?
- Do you need to ask your neighbors for permission before you start keeping hens, and if so, what information or documents do you need as proof?
- Do you require any licenses to raise chickens or construct a coop?
- If you can't have chickens, are you willing to band together with other chicken lovers to highlight the benefits and organize community support to see if your local regulations can be changed?
- If you intend to keep hens for eggs and meat, can you butcher them where you live? City health regulations will govern the slaughter of chickens, and the slaughter of any animal may be forbidden.

Next-Door Neighbors

I recommend speaking with your neighbors and informing them of your plans before getting hens. Discuss the advantages. You can tell your neighbors that hens are peaceful and will not cause any problems. If keeping animals offends your neighbors, some localities have nuisance laws prohibiting you from doing so. It's an obvious point to make, but people move residences, and while your current neighbors may be excellent, you never know who might move in next.

Obey All Other Laws

You must comply with all other rules, including those regarding noise, sanitation, and animal care.

REQUIREMENTS FOR SPACE

After you've determined the rules in your area regarding raising hens, you'll need to evaluate the space requirements for your venture. You don't need a lot of room or space if you're not planning on having hens on a considerable scale. However, it would be best if you first answered the following questions before determining the amount of room required to rear your chickens:

- Would you like your chickens to be free to roam during the day?
- How many chickens will you keep?
- How long do you want your chickens to stay in their coops during the day?

Answering these questions will assist you in determining how much space you require. However, before we answer these questions, remember that your coop should be as large as possible. (Once you have invited these animals into your life, I guarantee you will want more. You will not know how you went into your feed store for a new waterer and came home with a few baby chicks, or more, instead.) A larger enclosure will prevent you from having to constantly expand when you add to your flock on purpose or not. Small spaces will also allow excrement to quickly build up, releasing a lot of ammonia into the atmosphere, which is hazardous for you and your chickens. Your chickens may become more agitated and peck at each other in close quarters, resulting in sickness, infections, and even death. Whatever you do, strive to make your enclosure as large as possible.

Three to six birds might be an excellent place to begin if you're starting with your backyard poultry farm. The ideal daily routine for a healthy and happy flock is for your hens to be allowed to explore freely during the day and stay in their coop at night. They can forage in the grass and then sleep restfully, protected from predators at night.

A flock of six chickens requires roughly 18 square feet for the coop and a run of about 60 square feet. So, you'll need at least 78 square feet to keep six chickens. This calculation is only the minimum space required for six chickens; you can do more. You may easily house your chickens in a coop if you have an area measuring 11 feet by 10 feet.

As mentioned earlier, a chicken coop (cage) should be around 3 square feet per fowl. For example, you have six chickens, so the enclosure should be roughly 18 square feet.

If you reside in a colder climate, you should be cautious about oversizing your coop. Having a large enclosure with only a few chickens inside may not be the best idea since the chickens will be unable to generate enough heat to keep themselves warm during the winter season. In colder climates, stick to around 3 square feet per bird rather than going much larger.

Of course, your hens will need a place to sleep and perch. Each bird will require around 10 inches of perching space. That means six birds would require a 60-inch perching spot (5 feet). Even though hens cuddle together at night, they still need enough perching space to keep their distance from one another and to maintain a suitable temperature. Comfortable chickens are happy chickens, and happy chickens produce better eggs and meat.

Finally, hens require a minimum of 15 square feet of space to wander. Did I mention how much chickens like roaming? They do, and if you can let them wander, you should! Regardless, six chickens would require approximately 90 square feet of running room within the coop. You could give them more space than this, and they would appreciate it.

TIME CONSTRAINTS

The simple part is getting your first flock of chickens. The tricky part is ensuring they have everything they require to be comfortable. You must guarantee that your birds have access to food, water, warmth, safety, and hygiene. Providing all of these can be time-consuming at first, so consider whether you have the time to care for your hens properly. It's not uncommon for people to sell their hens because they no longer have time to look after them. Like other domesticated animals, chickens cannot be left to fend for themselves. Therefore you should set aside enough time for them.

If you don't have much time but still want to start your flock, consider hiring a neighborhood youngster to help you keep an eye on your hens and tend to their needs, or perhaps a neighbor will help in exchange for some fresh eggs.

COST CONSTRAINTS

Another issue to consider before ordering some chickens is the expense. You must first determine how much money you can afford to spend and if that will be enough to invest in these birds to accomplish your purpose for them. Raising hens is a fantastic way to be self-sufficient while possibly also making some money on the side.

There are numerous factors to consider in this situation. Consider how many hens you want to raise, whether you want to raise them for meat or eggs, and the cost of feed and supplies like coops and feeders. You must also decide whether it is cheaper to grow your chickens or buy eggs and meat from a poultry farmer or a grocery store.

You can use the following inventive methods to help you save money and cut costs:

- Add grains to the bird feed.
- Allow your chickens to roam freely in the yard.
- Provide them with kitchen scraps
- Offer extra eggs and chicks for sale.
- Sell elderly laying hens or use them for meat.
- Prefer light breeds over hefty breeds.

You must also create a budget for how much you anticipate spending. It's worth noting that raising pullets to
the point where they start laying eggs takes around five
months. Broiler chickens take approximately eight
weeks to reach a size worth the meat they produce.

The next stage would be to choose your chicks once
you've finalized your budget and are sure you're ready
to start. The following chapter will assist you in
choosing the correct breeds and identifying sick or
weak chicks so that you can avoid as many problems as
possible when starting your new flock.

HOW MANY CHICKENS DO YOU REQUIRE?

Chickens are incredibly social birds, to the point that
they require a companion to keep them happy. You
should have at least two chickens to accommodate this
need. Most publications recommend having two hens
per family member, primarily to cover the number of
eggs you'll need to feed your household and to share
the responsibility of their care.

WHICH CHICKEN BREEDS SHOULD YOU RAISE?

There are around 400 different chicken breeds. As a
result, choosing which type of chicken to raise in your

flock can be difficult. Fortunately, there are questions you can answer to help you narrow down your options. You will get a rundown of the most popular breeds in the next chapter, so hold on.

Which Is Better: Standard or Bantam Chickens?

Standard chickens, often known as substantial fowl chickens, are chickens of average size. On the other hand, bantam chickens are significantly smaller than ordinary chickens. They're generally kept as pets because they're tiny and can be mixed in with a flock of standard-sized chickens. They also lay less regularly than other hens, but their eggs are still edible despite their diminutive size.

Most people prefer standard-sized chickens because of their larger body size and eggs. They're also less sensitive to predators, making them easier to rear than bantams.

Which Chickens Can Withstand the Cold?

Another aspect that will most likely influence the type of chicken you grow is the weather. Certain breeds thrive in colder climates while others in warm climates. Standard chickens, for example, are far hardier than bantam chickens and can survive colder temperatures. Due to their build, heavier breeds like Plymouth Rocks,

Langshans, Sussexes, Chanteclers, and Wyandottes do well in those long winter months.

Which Chickens Can Withstand the Heat?

Some chickens do better than others in warmer climates. Avoid larger, fluffier, or feather-footed chicken breeds if your area regularly encounters temperatures of 100 degrees or higher.

White Leghorns, Light Brown Leghorns, and Golden Campines are common breeds that thrive in warm regions. Because these varieties are native to Mediterranean climates, they can adapt to the heat wherever.

What About Egg Production?

There are chicken breeds that are better suited for meat production, and there are breeds that are more equipped for laying eggs. If you're only planning on getting hens for egg production, as most backyard farmers do, you want to purchase an egg-laying breed. Next, you will have to decide what color and quantity of eggs you desire and their behavior before deciding on any specific breed or breeds.

How well your hens respond to you and your other family members will ultimately be determined by their level of human interaction conditioning. White Leghorns, for example, are known to be nervous and avoid human interaction. Their temperaments should be considered, but also remember that everyone's experience with raising chickens is different! Rhode Island Reds, Stars, and White Leghorns are some of the top egg-laying breeds. Orpingtons, Marans, Australorps, Wyandottes, and Plymouth Rocks are all dual-purpose breeds that lay eggs.

Should You Start with Chicks or Young Hens?

Most individuals begin with young hens, sometimes referred to as starting pullets. The amount of work you're willing to put into rearing chicks or young hens will determine whether you start with chicks or young hens.

Raising young chicks is undoubtedly one of the greatest pleasures for chicken lovers. Remember that young chicks require the same level of attention as other infant animals. They're also quite impossible to find in small quantities. To give you an idea, many chicken breeders won't sell chicks in quantities of fewer than twenty-five; therefore, you might have to split an order with other backyard chicken growers in your neighborhood.

Always inquire about the number of chicks sold by chicken breeders and whether they can accommodate the number of chicks you want to raise. You don't want to have too many chicks at once since you won't be able to adequately care for them all. You might get lucky and find breeders that are ready to sell smaller batches of chicks.

Also, you should purchase sexed chicks or chicks whose sex has already been determined. You want female chicks who have been separated from male chicks, in other words. If you don't buy from a breeder who has sexed their chicks, you can end up with several males, and eventually have a lot more roosters than you want! Many times, when you receive your chicks, half of them end up being roosters. What makes it even more difficult is that you won't know if they are roosters until a few weeks afterward.

To Get a Rooster or Not?

A rooster isn't required to get eggs. If you're new to raising backyard hens, most chicken breeders advise against acquiring a rooster. Zoning rules, noise regulations, and other difficulties with neighbors are all significant concerns. After all, roosters sing all day long, not just in the morning, as many believe.

Experienced chicken handlers purchase roosters to protect their hens from predators and better govern the flock. Remember that owning a rooster requires a little more effort, so buy one only when you're sure you'll be able to care for him properly.

What Are the Best Places to Find Chickens?

Chicks can be purchased at a local farm supply store, but if your community has a bird hatchery, you're already ahead of the game. Searching for a specific breed may be a bit more work, but the internet is an excellent resource for precisely the proper chicken for your flock. Most of the time, you can reach out to them to learn more about what they offer.

How Do You Choose Your Breed of Chicken?

Choosing your breed of chicken can be complex to achieve your goals. So, researching all the chicken types you might desire in your backyard is always a smart idea. You start with the egg layers and narrow down the selection of egg layers by the other requirements you have.

Other concerns that affect your chicken choice are the number of eggs they can give you and the color of the eggs they produce. Furthermore, different breeds have various temperaments, adaptability, and noise levels. Those who live in cities or towns may choose a calmer breed, while those who live in rural settings are usually unaffected. Beginners should look for chickens roughly the same age to prevent adult birds from picking on smaller birds.

Standard chickens excel in egg production. Smaller bantam hens lay eggs, but they may not be sufficient for your nutritional requirements. If you require a lot of eggs, you'll want to consider how often your chickens lay. Some breeds have a slower rate of egg production. You'll need chickens that can keep up with your egg consumption rate. Most people do well with breeds with a medium egg production rate, but if you eat a lot of eggs, you may search for a different breed.

3

PICKING THE FLOCK

There are hundreds of chicken breeds to choose from when you purchase chickens. It would help if you considered the primary reason, you're buying them. Do you want the chickens for meat, eggs, pets, or to show off to your friends? Each breed has its personality and may require varying amounts of space. You should also make sure the hens are suitable for the climate where you reside. Rather than taking on too much at once, it is best to start in a modest way. As a result, choosing to start with a small flock of four to six chickens is wise.

All chicken breeds are classified into purebred, heritage, hybrid, and bantam.

Breeders or small farms carefully select purebreds or natural interminglings between wild breeds that result in the development of purebreds. Purebred chickens have distinct appearances and are given names based on their origins, such as Orpington, Leghorn, Andalusian, Dorking, etc. Purebred chickens used to have tremendous egg-laying abilities; however, current purebred hens are not quite as capable as egg-layers due to the desire to breed for show. Australorps, for example, were initially known to produce up to 350 eggs each year, but they now only lay about 250 eggs a year. Some individuals prefer purebreds because they have more personality than commercial egg-layers, live longer, lay for extended periods, and adapt to varied environments.

Purebred breeds include heritage breeds. The term "heritage breeds" refers to older breeds such as the Cochin. However, the terms "legacy" and "purebred" are frequently used interchangeably, and most people are unaware of the distinction.

Commercial layers, also known as hybrid breeds, are egg-laying machines. These breeds have been developed through thorough scientific selection and genetic engineering to optimize egg-laying qualities. They're also calm and don't take up a lot of room. However, they do not lay for long periods, usually around two years or less.

Bantam chickens are miniature chickens. They're about half to a third the size of conventional chickens. Their eggs are also around half the size of traditional eggs; in most recipes, two regular eggs equal three bantam eggs. If you don't have ample space, they're a great option. Bantam chickens are the offspring of all purebred chickens. There are also true bantams, which are only available in the size of a bantam and have no regular-sized counterparts.

FACTORS TO CONSIDER

Before we get into picking the proper breed, it's vital to consider a few key aspects that will help you figure out which breed is best for you and your environment.

Bird Size

Chickens come in various sizes; the larger they are, the more space they need. They are divided into three categories: large, standard, and bantam.

Chickens labeled as large are above 18 inches tall and weigh more than 10 pounds. Breeds including the Jersey Giant, Brahma, Orpington, and Australorp belong to this category. Unfortunately, many people are hesitant to maintain these massive birds because they appear menacing, yet most large breeds are calm and friendly. One of the significant advantages of their size is that they lay gigantic eggs.

Standard chickens range in height from 12 to 16 inches and weigh 5 to 10 pounds. Standard-sized breeds are often outstanding egg layers with a long lifespan. Rhode Island Reds, Plymouth Rocks, Wyandotte, and a variety of hybrids such as Golden Comets and Black Stars are among them.

Silkies are true bantam chicken breeds with no standard-size counterpart, whereas Leghorns are miniature variants of traditional chicken breeds. Bantam chickens rarely reach a height of more than 8 inches and weigh less than 5 pounds. Keep in mind that while bantam chickens are ideal for compact settings, they lay fewer eggs than regular chickens.

Temperament

The disposition of a chicken is also vital. You'll want hens who are easy to handle, or at the very least, tolerate humans. Some varieties dislike humans are flighty, and lay their eggs in hidden locations. If you want a pleasant, docile, peaceful chicken, avoid breeds known for fighting! Do your homework; you are the only person who understands what sort of hen you want.

Most backyard chicken enthusiasts desire a friendly and approachable flock and those that lay many eggs. Shy, aloof, and independent are all words that indicate this is not a pet chicken. Words like lively and entertaining are indicators that they may roost in trees. If you're shopping for hens for your kids to raise for 4H projects, keep in mind that some hatcheries sell chickens that aren't 4H friendly (read the fine print).

Space Requirements

You'll need to figure out how much space you have for a coop and a run before deciding on a breed. A typical breed requires at least 3 square feet per bird inside the pen. They will need at least 15 square feet per bird in the run if they are to be contained. Large breeds will require more space; for example, Jersey Giants will need 6 to 8 square feet of coop area and at least 20 square feet of outdoor space. Bantams, on the other hand, will require less space. Measure the area available for your coop and run to get a sense of the size of chicken you'll be able to raise and how many you'll be able to keep in your flock.

Climate

It's critical to find the proper breed for your location. Many overlook this issue; certain birds love heat and humidity, while others prefer a cooler, more temperate habitat. Chickens from warmer climates will struggle to survive in northern Minnesota without some warmth and protection. Matching your hens to their ideal environment will result in contented and healthy hens providing you with plenty of eggs. Orpingtons, Rhode Island Reds, and Brahmas are examples of chickens that can live in a warm area all year. Australorps, Silkies, or Plymouth Rocks are good choices if you live in a cooler climate.

Production of Eggs

Chickens of all breeds lay eggs, although they do so at varying rates and sizes. Your decision on which hens to buy may be influenced by the egg color or size, and the number of eggs you want.

CHOOSING THE RIGHT BREED FOR YOU

What you want to do with your hens will determine which breed is best for you. Do you want chickens that will provide you with many eggs for your family or to sell? Would you like to have chicken meat readily available for a meal? Are you looking for the companionship of a pet such as a hen in your home? Or do you want a unique chicken to show? Some hens, like Faverolles, have feathered feet; others, like Ameraucanas, have beards; and Polish chickens have odd hairdos.

There are plenty of breeds of chickens to pick from, including Silkies, Russian Orloffs, Silver-Laced Wyandottes, and many more. Most people love having a variety of chicken breeds in one flock. One of the appealing things to chicken keepers is that you don't have to stick to just one kind; hens of all varieties usually get along well. This will also mean having an assortment of colorful eggs.

A hot climate is generally one with temperatures above 100°F. Penedesencas, Leghorns, and Andalusians are some Mediterranean breeds that enjoy warmer temperatures. These hens are sleek, tiny, and have colossal combs to keep cool.

If you reside in a cold area, hens with larger bodies and smaller combs, such as Wyandottes, Barred Rocks, Cochins, Buff Orpingtons, and Australorps, would be the best choice. Because they have thicker coats, chickens with a lot of feathers will do better in cooler weather. In the winter, it's better to stay away from feather-legged chickens since muck and slush can stick to their legs and cause frostbite. If you reside in a cold environment, you can apply Vaseline to the combs and wattles of the birds to help avoid frostbite.

BEST BREEDS FOR EGGS

The most significant advantage of rearing backyard chickens is having a constant supply of fresh eggs; retrieving from the birds' nesting boxes each morning brings such enjoyment and pride. While it may seem self-evident, most newcomers are unaware that the breed of chicken you choose remarkably impacts the number of eggs you can expect. For a continuous supply of fresh eggs throughout the year, selecting the appropriate breed is critical; thus, here are the best egg-laying chicken breeds:

Leghorn

Known initially as Italians, they were eventually renamed Leghorns. The ancestral line of this breed can be traced back to Tuscany; however, the actual origin of what we now name the Leghorn is unknown. It arrived in the United States in the 1800s and is now one of the most common breeds in modern industrial egg production. While most people associate the Leghorn with white feathering and a red comb, they come in various hues. Regardless, the white feathering on these birds has made them one of

America's most recognizable breeds. The Leghorn is a very clever animal that has proven to be self-sufficient. It can find a considerable portion of its food if given the option to free range. They may choose to roost in a tree after enjoying a day foraging in the yard.

Because they are high-energy birds, the more room they have, the better, they are known for becoming noisy if bored and cooped up for too long. This breed also has a longer egg-laying lifespan, which benefits you. They make excellent starter hens but are challenging to educate, so avoid this breed if you want to tame your birds.

Leghorns have a yearly egg production of roughly 250–300. Their eggs are medium-sized and white. They have full white bodies and substantial, thick red combs, making them attractive birds. White Leghorns are a good choice for someone starting a flock.

Rhode Island Red

Red chickens are dual-purpose chickens, meaning they can be raised for eggs as well as meat. They originated in America. Because they are considered outstanding foragers, they make excellent free-range birds and penned hens, if the pen is moved around frequently enough to provide adequate fodder. Because they are tough and lay many eggs, they are one of the most popular chicken breeds.

A Rhode Island Red chicken lays 250 eggs each year on average. Their eggs are brown and modest in size. Despite their name, Rhode Island Reds have brown and black feathers that give them a dull appearance. They are recognized for their toughness and ability to take care of themselves. They are popular among first-time chicken keepers because they are quite personable.

Sussex

Like the Rhode Island Red, the Sussex is a dual-purpose breed, which can be raised for eggs and meat. In a year, a Sussex hen can easily lay 250 eggs. The color of their eggs will range from brown to creamy white. The most prevalent color combination for the Sussex breed is a pure white body with black neck and tail feathers.

They are peaceful chickens who would contentedly feed in a garden without causing damage. The Sussex is an excellent choice if you want a gentle breed that will eat from your hand and display a submissive disposition.

Golden Comet

There are numerous hybrid breeds, with Golden Comet being one of the most popular. Hybrids have been bred to lay countless eggs while eating a small amount of food, making them less expensive to feed than other breeds. Golden Comet chickens lay roughly 280 eggs each year. Their eggs are ordinarily brown in color and modest in size. Golden Comets have silky white tail feathers and are often golden-brown in appearance. They are robust and sturdy birds who rarely go broody. Golden Comet is a terrific choice if you're searching for a reliable year-round egg layer that requires little care.

Red Sex Link

A prominent hybrid chicken breed is Red Sex Link. They're noted for their rapid growth and enormous brown egg production rate. Their one-of-a-kind benefit is that they can be separated by their predominant feather color on the day they hatch, making males and females easy to distinguish. You can be sure you're buying hens from a hatchery or a breeder when you buy Sex Links.

The Red Sex Link is a hearty free-range bird that lays about 250 eggs annually. Their eggs are brown in color and range in size from medium to giant. Red Sex Links are golden brown in hue, with white feathers around their necks, tails, and occasionally their entire bodies. They are not known for being aggressive; instead, they are calm hens who get along well with other birds.

They make excellent pets because of their laid-back nature; however, they are not particularly broody.

Australorp

Australorps are beautiful chickens that are also personable and are good egg layers. They handle confinement well but are better suited to a free-range lifestyle than other larger breeds. They can be challenging to grow with other breeds since they bully and sometimes consume the eggs of other birds. Please keep this in mind if you choose to raise them alongside other birds.

Australorps lay about 250 eggs every year on average. The eggs have a light brown hue and are medium in size. Australorps are stunning, with black feathers that have a beetle-green gleam. They are often added to a flock because of their unique feathers.

Plymouth Rock

The Plymouth Rock (Barred Rock) is an excellent choice for a newbie chicken keeper. They're one of the sweetest and friendliest hens you'll ever meet, and they get along great with other birds. They are also excellent foragers and egg layers.

A Plymouth Rock lays roughly 200 eggs annually, which are light brown and are large. The birds are usually gray with white stripes around their bodies.

They are giant birds that thrive in a free-range environment. They are, like the Sussex, gentle and amiable birds that are easily tamed.

Golden Laced Wyandotte

These large birds are stunning, and many purchase them only for their appearance. But their good looks aren't all they have going for them. They produce many eggs, are excellent foragers, and are kind and peaceful.

Golden Laced Wyandottes lay roughly 200 eggs every year. Their light-brown eggs range in size from medium to large. The chickens have dark brown or black backgrounds with golden lacing all over their bodies. They are calm, reserved, and excellent foragers, making them ideal free-range chickens.

New Hampshire Red

New Hampshire Reds were produced in New Hampshire and Massachusetts as a distinct strain of the Rhode Island Red breed. New Hampshire Red hens are resilient and broody.

They lay light brown tinted eggs that are medium in size. The feathers of New Hampshire Reds are a lighter shade of red than those of Rhode Island Reds. They are good layers but can get highly broody, which causes them also to be fantastic mothers. The number of eggs laid by New Hampshire Reds per year is roughly 200.

Buff Orpington

Buff Orpington hens are a breed of chicken that originated in Kent, England and make excellent backyard chickens. They are large, attractive birds that make excellent companions. They aren't the most prolific egg-layers, but their peaceful demeanor more than compensates, making them a favorite of many chicken keepers.

Buff Orpingtons lay roughly 180 eggs per year on average. Their feathers are a thick, beautiful golden-yellow color. This breed is very social, wanting to become a part of your family. You can easily teach them to feed from your hand.

Bantam Chickens

Bantam chickens are miniature chickens. Bantam chickens are the offspring of all purebred chickens. Bantams are not a breed; instead, the term relates to the size of the chicken, and there are several different bantam varieties. True Bantams, Miniaturized Bantams, and Developed Bantams are three.

True bantams evolved without the intervention of humans. They are naturally petite and do not have regular-sized counterparts. Rosecombs and Sebrights are two examples of real bantams.

Humans have created little bantams from existing regular-sized breeds such as Rhode Island Reds, Orpingtons, and others. Breeders mate a standard breed with a bantam breed resulting in chicks gaining the dominant gene for the smaller size, such as the Japanese, Pekin, and Cochin.

Bantam chickens are almost half the size of a conventional chicken, so they're a good option if you're short on room but still want to raise chickens. Their eggs are usually half the size of those laid by ordinary chickens, too. In most cases, three bantam eggs are equivalent to two regular-sized eggs. Naturally, they eat less and take up less room than conventional chickens. While a traditional chicken needs at least 3 square feet of indoor space, a bantam requires only 2 square feet.

In comparison to conventional chickens, they do not require any extra care. However, because they are smaller and have a faster metabolic rate, they easily feel chilly and do not do well in colder climates. To keep them warm, you can use a chicken coop heater. They can also fly better than conventional chickens, so you'll need slightly higher fencing—usually a foot taller than for regular chickens—despite their smaller size. You might want to clip their wings if they keep flying out of their run. Bantams can live among regular-sized chickens, although I don't encourage it. Due to their small size, they are sometimes bullied by the larger chickens.

If you want bantams for eggs, avoid the Japanese, Pekin, and Sebright kinds, as they only lay 50–80 eggs per year. The finest egg-laying bantam breeds are Easter Eggers and Araucanas, which may lay up to 280–300 eggs yearly. Brahmas and Cochins are also capable egg layers, laying over 200 eggs each year.

This book has provided information on a few of the hundreds of chicken breeds. It specifically focused on the most common egg-laying varieties for the purposes of this book. Please explore and gain more knowledge on all the unique breeds available to you.

WHAT AGE CHICKEN TO START RAISING

When you first start keeping chickens, deciding whether to buy eggs, chicks, or adult chickens might be difficult. The sections below will go over the advantages and disadvantages of the various options and will assist you in making an informed selection.

Egg Hatching

If you buy eggs, you'll need an incubator, which will keep the eggs at the right temperature and humidity for twenty-one days. You'll need to check the temperature and humidity, adjust as needed, and turn the eggs. Although not all eggs will hatch, watching the ones that do is a truly magical experience. If you're new to chickens, it's usually better to start with chicks and don't try hatching them until you are more experienced with chickens.

Chicks

You can buy chicks as young as a day old. When you get them, it's simple to form a bond with them by feeding, teaching, and petting them. Watching them mature into adult chickens who strut about your yard is fun.

When buying chicks, there are a few things to keep in mind. In their first few weeks of life, chicks require more attention. They will be contained in a brooder with a heat lamp to keep them warm and pine shavings and newspapers to line the floor. Make sure you have everything ready before the chicks arrive, as deliveries can sometimes arrive a day or two early.

Also, as distressing as it may sound, a chick or two may die during delivery. Be especially cautious if this is a new experience for you and avoid opening newly delivered chicks in front of children. Most hatcheries provide replacements or refunds, but it's not so much about the money as the disappointment of a living creature not making it. If you're ordering in this manner, you can always get a few more than you need to ensure you have the flock size you desire.

You can buy either straight run chicks (which are not sexed and will give you a mix of males and females) or sexed chicks (which will provide you just females for laying eggs). Even if you buy sexed chicks, there's a chance you'll get a male because sexing isn't foolproof. Some farms and farm stores will repurchase roosters. Refund and return procedures vary from retailer to retailer, so do your homework before purchasing poultry from one.

Here are the pros and cons of buying chicks to start a flock:

✛ Pros:

- Buying chicks allows you to bond with them and help them become social with people.
- Chicks have a low risk of contracting diseases due to environmental exposure.
- Chicks don't have any bad habits or behavioral issues.
- Marek's disease vaccines are available.
- They are far less expensive to buy than pullets.

― Cons:

- The cost of getting chicks to the laying stage can be more than buying pullets.
- They require extra attention for the first eight weeks after you receive them.
- Before they start laying eggs, you'll have to wait for them to mature and grow.
- Even with sexed chicks, purchasing a male chicken is always possible.

Pullets

A pullet is a name for a young chicken between 15 and 20 weeks old. Within this time, they will begin laying, but their eggs may be on the smaller side until they have been laying for a few months. Again, purchasing pullets can initially be more expensive than purchasing young chicks, but it is usually less costly than raising chicks until they are ready to lay. The benefits and drawbacks of buying pullets are as follows:

+ Pros:

- There isn't much of a wait before they start laying eggs.
- There is little chance of buying a male chicken by accident.

— Cons:

- You might not be able to bond as easily as you would with a chick.
- They may have certain undesirable habits and behaviors instilled in them already.
- There's a possibility of being tricked into buying older, less productive chickens.
- There is a chance of contracting infections due to environmental exposure.
- They cost more than a chick.

Adults

You can buy older hens ready to lay eggs if you don't want to wait 16 to 18 weeks for chicks to grow. Chicks require a lot of attention and are delicate, but mature hens need less of your time. The primary disadvantage of purchasing mature hens is that determining their age is difficult. Adult chickens are usually very productive egg layers during the first two years of their lives, but as they age, laying decreases. If you acquire older chickens, you have no idea what kind of conditions they were in for the first few months regarding nourishment and sanitation. Look into animal shelters or rescue sanctuaries if you want mature chickens.

✚ Pros:

- They'll start laying eggs right away.
- There's no danger in purchasing a male chicken.
- You may adopt hens for a reasonable price.

━ Cons:

- You might not be able to bond and socialize with your chicken.
- They may have certain undesirable habits and behaviors instilled in them already.
- It's impossible to tell how old a chicken is, so you'll have to trust the seller's word.
- There is a chance of contracting infections due to environmental exposure.

WHERE CAN I BUY CHICKENS?

Hatcheries

Day-old chicks can be ordered online or over the phone from hatcheries, and you can choose which breeds to add to your flock. Chicks are generally available from February to April and occasionally later into the spring and summer. Most hatcheries have a large breed selection, and some even take advance orders.

You may find hatcheries near you by searching online; choosing one nearest you is better so the babies don't have to travel far to get to you. Hatcheries can send you chicks through a mail service, or you can pick them up, allowing safe travel to your home. February to April is the best time to order because the temperatures are milder and more optimum for the chicks while shipping.

Feed Stores

Feed stores typically have reasonable prices, but the variety of breeds available is usually limited. Hatching eggs or day-old chicks may be available at feed retailers such as Tractor Supply Company. Most feed stores have minimum purchase requirements of four to six chicks at a time and don't have much information about them. They are cheap for a reason.

Farmers in the Area

Local farmers will sell hatching eggs, day-old chicks, and adult chickens. Generally, only specific breeds may be available, and they may not know the gender. Even if people don't sell chickens themselves at a farmers' market, they may have a friend who does.

Private Breeders

Chicken raising is a big business, so please do your homework. If you're buying from a private breeder, you should do thorough research immediately. Request some reviews from prior customers to verify the quality of their chickens. Trustworthy raisers are significantly better, so your chicks may be a little more expensive, but it is worth it for the peace of mind.

Festivals and Shows

People participating in poultry shows and displaying their birds at shows and fairs are knowledgeable. They put a lot of work and money into keeping the birds in tip-top shape. Although you will most likely be unable to purchase the award-winning bird, the proprietor may sell you a selection of other birds. The birds are usually endorsed by the NPIP (National Poultry Improvement Program) and have undergone sickness testing at these events.

Auctions

If you're new to the poultry world, keep in mind that closeouts aren't the best place to get high-quality stock. Animal sales in the neighborhood might range from excellent to disastrous. Animals are frequently traded and exchanged for a reason, which is not good. If you do take this path, I wouldn't recommend bartering unless you have someone experienced with you.

Poultry Clubs

If you encounter a local poultry club or meetings, take advantage of them! These people have been around chickens for much longer than you, so they have a lot of information to share. You'll soon discover that chicken people enjoy talking about their pets! They can undoubtedly direct you in the right direction regarding obtaining birds, and they may even sell you a few of their own.

HOW TO PICK YOUR CHICKENS

You should be aware of the signs of healthy and ill hens while picking chicks, pullets, or adults. Here are things to look for:

- A healthy hen should have bright, clear eyes free of discharge. Blindness or an underlying ailment is frequently indicated by cloudy eyes or a lack of attention.
- They should be awake and energetic, genuinely curious about their surroundings and you.

- Their feathers should be shiny and bright in color, and there should be no injuries or bald patches.
- When you pick up a chicken, it should be fat and heavy. If you can see the chicken's breastbone, it's likely malnourished and underweight.
- Examine the beak to ensure it isn't fractured or peeling away. It should be straight, not twisted or crossed. A broken beak does not always heal, and chickens with broken beaks have difficulty eating and drinking.
- Check to see if the vent is clean. If left untreated, a clogged vent can be fatal. Loose stools might build up around the vent, sealing it shut.
- Examine the legs to ensure they are straight and free of scaly patches. It could signify a leg mite infestation if they're scaly.

ESTIMATED COSTS OF STARTING A FLOCK

It's always a good idea to consider how much your chickens will cost you before obtaining them and plan for unexpected costs like more fencing, extra waterers, veterinary fees, and healthcare. The prices listed below are for a total of five chickens. Adjust these rates accordingly depending on how many chickens you have in your flock.

The higher the quality of the feed you give your chickens, the more eggs they will lay. If you feed your chickens standard feed, the cost per month will be roughly $30. However, if you choose non-GMO feed, this might cost up to $150 per month, which is a significant difference. You might wish to budget for black soldier fly larvae or mealworms, bee pollen, and rose petals in your treats. You may also want to provide them with herbal supplements, such as nesting herbs to help them maintain a healthy immune system. These herbs include chamomile, lavender, calendula, spearmint, dill, roses, and fenugreek.

Chicken coops come in a variety of prices. You may get one for around $200, but it may not be adequate and must be changed after a few years. So, before you buy hens, research the coop style you want and consider it in your budget because the coop is usually the most considerable upfront amount when establishing a backyard flock. You could build your pen if you're handy with tools and have extra wood on hand, or you could pay up to $2,000 for a custom chicken coop. Buying a garden shed to convert into an enclosure is a fantastic option because you can convert it back to a shed if you don't want to keep hens in the future.

Bedding costs roughly $20 per month on average. Feeders and waterers are usually relatively inexpensive. It's always a good idea to have a few extras on hand to ensure your chickens have a fair chance of getting food and water in case something goes wrong.

Most breeds of chicks cost roughly $5 each (females tend to be more expensive than males). It also depends upon the breed and whether it is a rare breed. Adult chickens can cost from $1 to $30 per pound. Pullets range in price from $15 to $25. Some chicken breeds are incredibly costly, such as the all-black Ayam Cemani, which may cost $5,000.

On average, five hens will cost you $70 a month over five years, including the coop, feed, bedding, and other costs, as well as the birds themselves. These costs do not include the savings of no longer needing to buy eggs from a store or selling eggs, meat, or birds. As a result, you may be able to recoup these expenses.

BRINGING YOUR CHICKENS HOME

If you've bought chicks, you'll need a brooding box to keep them in. The container must have high edges to prevent the chicks from escaping, as well as feeding and watering dishes.

Chicks are susceptible to cold drafts, so their home must be draft proof. To help the chicks stand, fill it with dry material such as pine shavings or paper towels. This surface will allow them to move around freely with traction to ensure the correct growth of their legs. A life-threatening condition can develop called spraddle leg or splayed leg if the ground is slippery. The babies will require warmth, so a heat lamp or an electric hen heat plate must be included in your brooder setup. They'll need to be warmed until they're 6 or 7 weeks old. Start with a temperature of 95°F and gradually lower it by 5°F each week until you achieve the desired temperature. If they cuddle together, it is a sign they are too cold. They may be too hot if you see them spread out along the edges of the box.

If you have a brooding box full of chicks in your residence, make sure that other creatures like cats and dogs can't access them. If you have youngsters who are prone to leaving doors open, consider installing a latch on the door that is high up and out of reach, preventing the door from being pushed open. Because chicks kick up dust and shed dander, keep them out of bedrooms, dining rooms, and kitchens if you suffer from allergies.

If you're going to raise chicks in an outbuilding, make sure it's predator-proof. Once the hens are permitted outside, the habitat must be predator-proof from hawks, owls, foxes, weasels, and raccoons, the most common predatory animals.

The following are the main points to remember from this chapter:

- Determine why you want hens to select the breed most suited to your needs.
- Think about suitable chicken breeds for your climate.
- Choosing an egg breed depends on your desired number of eggs, size, and color.
- You can buy eggs, chicks, pullets, or adults when purchasing chickens.
- Hatcheries, local farms, chicken breeders, and feed stores sell chickens.
- You might start small, with four to six chickens, and gradually expand your flock.
- A healthy chicken should have bright, clear eyes as well as straight legs and beaks, and be active and curious with a clean vent.
- The cost of five chickens over five years would be roughly $70 per month.

We will cover housing for hens in the next chapter, looking at the many available options. You don't want all your work of raising chickens to come to a tragic end as a predator finds a way into the coop at night, attacking and possibly killing your flock. This chapter examines whether you should buy or build a chicken coop. It will explain the necessary details of a coop, such as size, location, insulation, ventilation, storage places, nesting boxes, lighting, power, and other factors to consider while building a chicken coop. It will cover chicken runs and yards and how to keep them safe. Finally, it will go through how to use a fence to keep hens out of your garden areas and keep predators out of the coop.

4

HOUSING THE FLOCK

Now that you have decided to raise chickens on your property, you should have also chosen the breed of chicken you want for your specific reasons and double-checked that you're legally authorized to keep them where you live. It would help if you have also finalized your decision on the age of your chickens, how many, and where you'll purchase them. Now, we need to discuss how you will house them once they are yours. This chapter will examine the many alternatives available to you, chicken shelter concerns, and whether you should buy or build your coop. We will discuss chicken runs and yards and the critical fence required to keep your chickens safe and protect your garden from the chickens eating plants and scratching up dirt.

It will be a continual learning process to ensure that your chickens are healthy and happy in their new home. Chickens require areas where they may feed, take a nice dust bath, sleep safely, and be comfortable without disturbing others. They will live longer if they have a constant, secluded, clean home to lay their eggs in. Chickens will want a safe place to go when the sun goes down and where they can sleep until the morning. They should be kept warm, dry, and well-ventilated in their home. As you can only imagine, a well-ventilated coop is necessary due to the droppings being contained in this one central location. While a chicken coop may appear to be an expensive investment initially, it is a one-time expense that will pay for itself over time.

Including a storage area for supplies within the site of the run and coop is beneficial. It will make your life easier but make sure your food supplies are correctly sealed to keep out bugs, your flock, and predators. There are eight essential factors to consider when building a chicken coop and run area for your flock:

- The coop needs to withstand all types of weather.
- The coop must be spacious for your chickens.
- The coop needs ventilation to keep your chickens healthy.
- The coop must contain nesting boxes.

- The coop must have roosts of varied heights.
- The coop and run must be safe and secure to prevent predators from entering.
- The run area should allow the birds to free range, forage, and take dust baths.
- The run needs both shaded and unshaded areas. Chickens love to sunbathe.

IMPORTANCE OF HOUSING YOUR CHICKENS

The use of a chicken coop is essential for a variety of reasons. They are as follows:

- Using a chicken cage keeps your chickens safe from predators. The dangers of exposing chickens include the possibility of a single predator affecting your entire flock. You must lock the chicken coop at night and leave them to free range during the day. However, the run of your chicken coop should also be enclosed by a fence to keep them safe during the day.
- When you let your flock free range, their droppings will end up in your garden. These will act as fertilizer, improving the growth of your plants.
- You can collect one or two eggs from your coop per day from your birds. If you have numerous

chickens, you may be able to gather as many as a dozen eggs daily. Knowing when the eggs were laid will make you confident that they will always be fresher and healthier than the eggs sold in local grocery stores.

- Chickens can play an essential role in keeping your backyard clean and tidy. They will assist in eating the weeds in your garden. These garbage pickers will also consume fruit that falls from your trees or in your garden, preventing rotten fruits from attracting unwanted pests.
- Bugs may wreak havoc on your garden and make it unattractive. Chickens are a great strategy to keep bugs at bay.

CHICKEN HOUSING OPTIONS

Free-Range

The free-range method entails allowing the flock to graze freely in an outside run or garden during the day and confining them at night. It can be in a backyard, an open field, or a fenced pasture. It should be a safe, open space with plenty of natural food, sunlight, shaded areas, a suitable drainage system, and predator protection. Chickens that can wander freely are happiest in a natural environment where they can explore and exhibit their behaviors. Chickens have complete freedom of movement within the boundaries of the land.

If you prefer to raise your birds in a free-range habitat, you will reap many benefits, but you must be prepared to face some hurdles to keep your flock safe.

✛ Pros:

- Feed consumption is reduced when chickens can scratch and scavenge for delectable delicacies on their own. They spend their days exploring and foraging in the woods, eating bugs, tiny creatures, worms, and grass. They require less feed, which will help with costs.
- Eggs have a better flavor. As they wander the garden, free-range hens consume more natural, high-protein food, producing high-quality eggs with bright golden yellow yolks.
- Chickens are healthier and more active. So many activities keep them busy, so free-range chickens stay fit and maintain a healthy weight. Chickens are less susceptible to infections and parasites when they can roam freely throughout the day, as opposed to when confined all day and night. They also get a variety of foods, which helps them meet their daily nutritional needs.

- They get rid of insects and pests. Chickens enjoy chasing after their next meal. They forage and scratch around, consuming anything that catches their attention, including small snakes, spiders, and mice. They will help to keep insects and bugs from sneaking into your house because they will be gobbled up first.
- They are on the lookout for their grit. Chickens pick up pebbles, sand, and small rocks as they walk, which help break down the food they eat during the day. It means buying fewer natural rocks or grit to aid digestion.
- To keep mites, lice, and feather concerns to a minimum, chickens require a dust bath area. They make a dust bath for themselves. Free-range hens have easy access to dry soil for their daily dust bath. You can use a large pot or tray filled with sand and dirt. Repurposing discarded, unused tires into chicken baths is another excellent idea. To entice your chickens, paint them in a variety of colors.
- They help you out in the garden. After harvesting the produce, the chickens will gladly till your garden beds for you. They also leave feces all over the place, naturally nourishing the soil. You may build a compost area and use this natural fertilizer to help your plants thrive.

- They take up less space in the coop. Allowing the chickens to range freely during the day reduces their urge to stay inside. They would only use the pen to sleep, eat, and lay eggs.

— **Cons:**

- They could consume undesirable and dangerous foods. Chickens will devour anything that appeals to them, including flower petals, herbs, and garden plants. Before letting your chickens out, make sure your garden is chicken-proof. Keep them protected from any pesticides, weed killers, and chemical fertilizers used on your plants.
- Predators find it easy to prey on your flock at any time. During the day, eagles, hawks, and domestic pets (dogs and cats) can strike anytime. During the night, your flock will be vulnerable to predators like raccoons, coyotes, foxes, weasels, bears, possums, and other creatures.
- They destroy your manicured areas. Keep chickens out of your garden since they enjoy scratching and dusting in the holes.
- They make a racket when they're locked up. Chickens are creatures of habit; they fuss and

make unpleasant noises to indicate their discontent when you don't let them go out at the designated time.

- Getting your chickens to poop in a specific spot is tough, and they'll do it whenever and wherever needed. As a result, expect their dung to be sprinkled around their outdoor run. They leave crap all over the place.

It's critical to build a stable, ventilated, large shelter for your chickens that keeps them safe from predators, parasites, and infections. A coop accommodates the flock's safety, bad weather, brooding, or egg-laying throughout the night. You also have the option of a movable chicken house with field units or mobile folds.

Many chicken keepers use a movable chicken coop to make different areas available for the hens to free range on the property. The first step is determining the stocking density concerning the pasture management method and soil type. If you live in an area where it rains a lot all year, ensure your shelter has an elevated and strong floor with a large overhang roof. For this, you can utilize a raised bamboo or solid soil platform. The elevated bamboo enables ventilation underneath, which is excellent in hot weather. Both alternatives keep them out of harm's way in the event of a flood.

This system's housing is less expensive than building a chicken coop. It can be self-contained, making it suitable for either intense or semi-intensive production processes. You can use mud or bamboo and bamboo slats for doors and windows for walls.

A well-managed free-range system will provide you with an abundance of healthy, fresh eggs.

Here's what you need to do:

- Establish a base of operations. It is vital to let your hens get acclimated to being in a limited space or housing before releasing them and allowing them to roam freely in your backyard while motivating them to return later in the evening to sleep and rest. You can use treats to entice the chickens back inside the housing during the day.
- Enclose your new garden plots and plants with a fence. Chickens enjoy tender and young flower stalks or plants as a delicacy. The sight of freshly mulched and dug garden soil is enticing to them, so make sure you have a sturdy fence between it and them.
- Keep them safe from a variety of predators. If your hens need to flee from cats, dogs, raccoons, hawks, eagles, or other predators,

ensure they have easy access to their shelters. Another option is to get a rooster to protect them in the event of an attack.

- Ensure that fresh, clean water is always available. Set up several drinking stations throughout the space to keep the chickens hydrated, especially during the hottest time of the day when they are out exploring and seeking food.

Cages

Hens can be kept in cages and stored in a barn or garage. Others options can include either hanging them from tree branches or connecting them to the edges of your building's outside wall surfaces. All options are feasible for a time but not a permanent home for your chickens. You should have one or two available for an injured or sick chicken to rest away from the flock.

When building or purchasing a chicken cage, you have two options for floor covering: wire or solid flooring. Cages constructed of wire mesh enable the option of various dimensions while keeping a minimum of 2 square feet per chicken. Chickens do well in cages if there is enough room to stand up.

✚ Pros:

- Keeping hens in cages helps you get them ready to reproduce.
- If you plan to show your chickens, keeping them in cages will help them become accustomed to the restricted space.

━ Cons:

- Wire floor coverings can hurt the chickens' toes if the wire bottom isn't built according to standard dimensions.
- Chickens kept in cages do not get enough exercise.

When is it the best idea to use a cage? Cages may be your only option if you simply want to maintain a few chickens and have a small space to keep them in. Because cages are housed or hung outside, you must ensure that the chickens are protected from extreme weather conditions and predators.

The biggest problem with cages is the flooring because it doesn't accommodate the little feet of chickens. Their feet slip through the holes, and toenails can get stuck, so the size of the gaps on the cage's flooring should not exceed 1.5 inches. When the hens try to flee, their legs or toes may be harmed or even injured. Limit the risk of injuries by using durable, heavy-duty flooring. Wire floor covering is only suitable for bantams and other small breeds weighing less than 5 pounds.

Allow your hens to walk about in your fenced yard when it's time to clean the cages. This will give them some exercise and time to forage. It may take some treats to get them back into the cages.

Unlike larger breeds, bantam chickens thrive in cages since they require less space.

The Run Area

As the name implies, it's a more spacious, fenced area for your flock to run. In this area, they forage and explore but are confined to that specific area, unlike free ranging. The coop is usually contained within the outdoor run area where they can walk freely without fear of being attacked by predators.

+ Pros:

- It's a solution for poultry keepers concerned about predators.
- It offers security while allowing them to be outside in the sun and fresh air.

— Cons:

- A significant amount of room will be required to safely leave your chickens in your backyard.
- It can be costly to construct at first.

A Tractor for Chickens?

Hen tractors are movable chicken enclosures that typically have two or four wheels. It will be easier for you to move around if it has more wheels. Chicken tractors come in a variety of shapes and sizes. While some will be less than 10 feet wide, others can be more than 15 feet across, allowing even more chickens to be housed. Hen tractors are unique in that they do not have a floor. It has a wood structure with lightweight wall surfaces. They can include nesting boxes; many feature conventional necessities, such as water, feed, and a roost. The hens can be moved to any region of the yard. The chickens roam freely inside the shelter, protected from the elements and predators.

+ Pros:

- Neither pellets nor grains can meet all of the chickens' nutritional needs. Allowing them to travel throughout the entire backyard, on the other hand, aids them in identifying and consuming calcium-rich insects. As a result, this aids in producing solid eggshells while supplying all the necessary nutrition for your hens.

- Because the chicken tractor is mobile, you can move it around to provide plenty of heat and sunlight throughout the cold months. You can move it in the summer to provide the necessary shade from the sun.

- Your garden is fed naturally because the manure contains a lot of phosphorus and nitrogen. Natural manure can also help you save money on plant food.

- You can quickly move the hens around the vegetable beds so that they can clean up the fallen, rotting food.

- Building a hen tractor from scratch can save money. Using recycled materials like wooden pallets, fencing, and plastic pipe while not breaking the bank.

- A chicken tractor provides constant fresh air, making your flock less susceptible to infections.

- Due to the tractor's mobility, hen feces will not gather in one spot. Once one area is covered by excrement, move the tractor.

▬ Cons:

- A hen tractor is not as solid and long-lasting as a stationary coop. A permanent enclosure will withstand various weather extremes, including hail, winds, snow, and sleet.
- A less fortified tractor will probably fail to protect hens from predators—a crucial consideration for every chicken keeper.
- Without extra work, the chicken tractor may not last through the seasons. You'll need to service it during the winter to provide additional chicken protection. You will have to bring it inside in severe weather to minimize damage to the tractor.

BASIC COOP REQUIREMENTS

Space for Your Hens

Birds must have enough space to coexist happily and are more likely to engage in anti-social behaviors such as plucking and pecking if they are crowded together. Winter is the worst season for these behaviors because hens become bored.

Standard birds require 3 square feet of coop area and 10 square feet of run space, while larger breeds require a coop of 5 square feet and a run of 15 square feet for each chicken. Although they usually hang together at one end, it's also recommended that each bird have 1 square foot of roosting area. Smaller birds, such as bantams, require less space than larger birds.

The winter season, as previously mentioned, is the most problematic, and they'll require adequate space inside the coop to have their own space. During the mild months of the year, your flock will only be sleeping in the coop at night, so the square footage of the enclosure can be slightly reduced. If the more timid flock members want to hide away or be alone, you should be able to supply them with quiet areas. The more space you offer them, the fewer problems you will have with your chickens.

Nesting Boxes

If you wish to collect eggs quickly from your chickens and not go on a hunt, nesting boxes must be included in your coop design. Hens prefer to lay their eggs in a dry, dark location. You'll need one nesting box for every three to five chickens, even though they will always seem to pile up in a couple of them, leaving the other nesting boxes vacant. A suitable nesting box should be at least 14 inches wide by 14 inches deep, with enough space for your hens to stand up.

Nesting boxes should be a couple of feet off the ground. Your chickens will lay their eggs in these by jumping up into them. Keep the nesting boxes below the height of the roosts to prevent your birds from roosting in them. If your chickens roost in your nesting boxes at night, consider closing them off. The chickens will become accustomed to using their roosts and stop using the nesting boxes after a few weeks. You don't want your chickens to make a mess by roosting on top of the nesting box. The best method to avoid this is to construct a box with a slanted roof. Your chickens will not be able to hop up onto a slope of 45 degrees.

Your chickens will require comfy nesting material to lay their eggs. Straw is a traditional sleeping material, but it isn't ideal because it becomes soggy and retains moisture which can lead to mold and mildew issues, especially in humid conditions. However, it's a cost-effective option that won't break the bank, and the chickens seem to enjoy it because it's easy to shape. Corn husks or dry wood shavings work well as nesting material, and they're easy to clean and don't retain as much moisture as straw and hay. Your chickens will kick it all over the place, no matter what kind of nesting material you use. There's no point in spending lots of money on bedding that will end up dispersed all over the coop floor.

Roosts

A roost is a location where your chickens can sit and sleep when they wish. When it's time to roost, most chickens will seek the highest position in the coop, so make sure your roost is more elevated than everything else. Your chickens may wind up roosting in your nesting boxes if they are at the same level as or above your perch. Your roosts should be at least 2.5 feet off the ground but no higher than 4 feet. Older chickens will have difficulty jumping up to them if they are too high. Your chickens will seek other areas to roost if the ceiling is too low. Your chickens should be able to roost at night if you provide enough roosting space. As mentioned before with crowded nesting boxes, they may get aggressive over the best roosting spot, so it is better to have many different perches available. Most breeds require 6 to 8 inches of roosting area width per hen.

The most frequent material used to construct roosts is wood. As roosts, I've seen folks use 2x4s, 2x2s, tree branches, and even pallets with a few slats removed. The 2x2s are suitable for smaller chicken breeds, while the 2x4s are best for larger, heavier chickens. If you use tree limbs, keep in mind that the gaps and crevices in the branches can serve as mite hiding places. Treating your roosts with neem oil can prevent mites from living in them.

Ensure that your roost is well-supported. Depending on the breed, a single hen might weigh anywhere from 2 to 10 pounds. If you have ten chickens, your roost may need to support up to 100 pounds of weight.

Because chickens poop often at night, keep the roosts away from nesting boxes, food, and water. When it's time to clean the coop, a "poop board" might make your life easier. It is a board that sits beneath the roost and collects the feces of the chickens. Build a poop board with a lip and fill it with sand if you use one. To clean it, simply use something to sift the poop out of the sand, like how you would clean a cat's litter box.

A hanging poop board may be required if your chickens are walking through the dung board and scratching around in the sand. Hang it from the roof with wires or chains, so it swings around if they jump on it, which usually prevents them from jumping on the board. This is not guaranteed, though; some chickens love a good swing.

Ventilation

Chickens excrete a lot of moisture, and their feces include ammonia, which can fill a coop with odors when closed. A well-ventilated coop will have enough openings to let moisture, heat, fumes, and humidity escape before they can build up and cause problems.

Chickens exhale water vapor in the same way that people exhale it. Chickens do not pee, which may come as a surprise to you. Instead, they expel excess moisture with their excrement. If the chickens are kept in a dry, ventilated coop, they are impervious to the cold. When a chicken is housed in a wet, cold coop, you expose it to various health issues, not the least of which is frostbite. A damp chicken coop may quickly become a sickly home. While you may think you don't want your coop to be drafty in a chilly region, ventilation is crucial in these conditions.

Leaving chicken feces in a poorly ventilated coop raises the ammonia level in the air and quickly causes lung problems. Allowing these fumes to sit in your chickens' home might create significant respiratory difficulties and make them more susceptible to illness and disease. A well-ventilated coop will feature several ventilation slots and holes that let air flow freely. Because warm air rises, placing vents at the top of your coop can assist in keeping air circulating throughout it, especially during the hot summer months.

Make sure your vent openings are covered with hardware cloth, wire mesh, or some other form of predator-proof material. Air should be able to flow freely through your coop while securely keeping predators out at the same time.

When you cut your vent holes, you'll want to figure out how to close them securely when you're not using them. During the winter, a hinged panel can be caulked shut to keep drafts out. You can block off the vents you don't need to keep the weather out and give a more pleasant atmosphere for your chickens during extreme weather or when it's frigid. The only vents you will keep open when it's cold outside are the ones at the top of your coop. These vents will keep the air fresh and avoid moisture buildup, but they will not create a chilly draft that will be uncomfortable for your hens.

Location

You must be able to tend to your chickens in all weather conditions; thus, it must be easily accessible. If you reside in an area with a lot of snow, the coop should be tall so that you can clean it even if it is snowing heavily. A shady place is ideal for preventing the coop from overheating in the summer. It can face south, with windows on the east and west sides, allowing your chickens to enjoy some sun.

Sunlight kills bacteria in the coop and dries out ammonia. It is also helpful to ensure that there is appropriate drainage in case rain gets in and causes pooling. A muddy hen is not happy and it can lead to parasites and infections.

Insulation

In the summer, coops should be cool, and in the winter, they should be warm. A good flow of air is required to keep the space ventilated but not so drafty that it causes chills. If you were building the coop yourself, ideally, you would place insulation in your walls like your own home. Since that is rarely the case, you can use cardboard, old fabric, burlap bags, or straw to insulate the coop. Each insulation method has pros and cons, so you must figure out what will work best for your chickens.

Flooring

A dirt floor, a timber floor, or a concrete floor are all good options. If you have a dirt floor, predators and rodents can dig their way in, so you'll need to bury fencing around the coop to keep them out. If you choose a wooden floor, be aware that it will absorb moisture and allow mites to infest the enclosure. Concrete flooring is ideal because it is easy to maintain and repels predators and mites but is hard. Many people have been known to lay vinyl flooring to give the hens a little more cushioning and comfort while in the coop.

Bedding

You can use various bedding materials as litter for your flock in the coop. They all have advantages and disadvantages.

- If you reside in a colder climate, straw is a good option for keeping chickens warm. It tends to stink and is challenging to clean; because it is not very absorbent, moisture will fall to the floor underneath and the straw must be replaced frequently.
- Wood shavings: Pine and cedar shavings are readily available and are offered at feed stores. They tend to be more expensive than other types of bedding. Depending on the brand, they might be dusty and can cause respiratory issues. Shavings are usually used because of the high absorption rate, making them simple to clean and providing reasonable odor control.
- Sand: Although sand is a time-consuming type of litter to control, users swear by it. It's frequently used with the deep-litter approach (more on that later), and it's turned, which means you turn it to move the clean sand from the bottom to the top when it becomes filthy. It clumps like cat litter and can be used by chickens for dust bathing. It's also effective at

removing odors. However, it does not compost and cannot be used as a fertilizer. It can also be dusty and offers less padding, resulting in a harsher landing for your hens when they jump from the roosts and nesting boxes.

- Recycled paper: Some people use paper, but I would save it for the brooder box instead. Although it takes a lot of paper to cover the entire coop, it's ideal for chicks in a brooder box because it's soft and delicate. While it absorbs quickly, it needs to be changed frequently, so you'll have to clean your coop often. It also doesn't help with odor management.

There are two methods for dealing with bedding. Let's start with the non-deep-litter method before moving on to the deep litter method. You would remove the old bedding and replace it weekly with your routine coop cleaning if you used the non-deep-litter method. If you have a small flock, you can do it every two weeks or monthly, but cleaning your coop and changing the bedding once a week is recommended.

Using the deep litter approach, you layer new bedding on top of the old, resulting in a compost pile with chicken excrement at the bottom. The deep-litter method is easier to handle than weekly bedding changes, forming a compost pile in the coop and retaining heat, which is beneficial if you live in a colder region.

The best scenario would be to use pine shavings for the deep litter method. Start with 4 to 6 inches of pine shavings. Then, flip the bedding every week and add another level of new bedding. The environment will determine the decomposition rate you reside in, the number of hens you have, how often you turn the litter, and how moist the coop is. The enclosure should not stink and should not have an ammonia odor. You should add more bedding and turn it frequently if it smells like manure.

You should clean the bedding once it reaches a height of around a foot. Some people clean it to bring the litter level back to 4 to 6 inches, while others clean it thoroughly. Leaving some litter will help the next batch get started. If you're employing the deep litter method, don't put diatomaceous earth (DE) inside the coop. It's a drying chemical that prevents the litter from composting by drying it out.

Lighting/Electricity

Having power in a chicken coop allows you to utilize heat lamps to keep your chickens comfortable in the cold or fans to keep them cool in the heat. Artificial light can also assist hens in continuing to lay eggs during the shortened daylight hours of winter. Unless you are an electrician, it is best to have the power installed by a professional to avoid fire hazards with extension cords, rodents gnawing through wires, or other issues.

Temperature

In high heat, chickens can become lethargic and over-heated. On the other hand, they don't enjoy it when it's too cold outside and they can get frostbite. They prefer a temperature of roughly 72°F because their body temperature is 105° to 106°F.

Feeders and Waterers

You'll need a lot of waterers and feeders that you can get to easily and that are at a height where the hens won't get poop in them. Provide two in the coop and two in the run, depending on the number of chickens in your flock. They can become very territorial over the water (or feeder), so if one is being guarded so the others cannot get water (or feed), another is available to the other chickens.

Hammock or Droppings Board

Collecting dung is significantly more manageable with a droppings board or hammock. You can remove either from the coop for quick cleaning, which will probably lengthen the time between your full coop cleanup days.

Dust Bath

Taking a dust bath keeps parasites to a minimum. A dust bath in the coop and run is essential, and it can be as simple as a kiddie pool or old tire full of sand they can use whenever they want. It is crucial during the winter months when they don't have as much access to a run or when there is snow and ice on the ground. The dust bath within the run must be covered to keep out the rain which can cause it to become muddy.

Doors

Automatic doors are available for purchase and installation, though they are generally not recommended. It's critical to double-check that all your chickens are inside and to do a quick health check on your birds. If they aren't all in, it could mean that one or more of them is sick or injured. Automatic doors can potentially trap a chicken out or allow a predator or a rodent to be trapped inside. They can fail, but a manual door with a lock will not.

PREDATOR PROTECTION

The most critical purpose of housing chickens is to protect them from predators and rodents. As a result, you'll need to know what kinds of predators and rodents are in your area. This knowledge will aid you in deciding on the structure and security elements for your coop.

It is impossible to inform you about all the predators you'll encounter, but I can only try. The types of predators in a given area vary depending on its location, population, and geographic profile.

Predators may not necessarily eat your hens or eggs, but they are unwelcome guests. They come scavenging for the chicken feed and, in the process, give your flock a scare, making them skittish for the next few days. They may contaminate the feed and your coop with their excrement, causing a possible disease outbreak. Some of them are infested with lice, fleas, and mites, which cause stress in your chickens and lower egg production.

Dealing With Predators

A few more safeguards you may take besides the coop structure:

- Secure your feeder within the run or coop to prevent these predatory animals from accessing it.
- If you're storing feed for a while, keep it in airtight containers such as feed drums.
- Ensure no spilled feed is in your coop to draw the predators, especially at night.
- Also, because rats and snakes like to eat your eggs, collect them before sunset, as they are more active at night.

Knowing the Predators in Your Area

Wildlife used to live in their natural habitats. Due to a growing population, many have lost their homes and are now congregating in metropolitan areas. The most prevalent predators are cats, dogs, coyotes, bobcats, foxes, raccoons, weasels, skunks, possums, snakes, and birds of prey (hawks, owls, etc.). Mammals, reptiles, and birds are the three types of chicken predators.

Before you dismiss this by saying, "I live in the city," keep in mind that these predators have a way of sniffing out and preying on chickens regardless of how crowded the area is. As a result, it would be ideal if you take proper precautions to safeguard your birds.

If you've lived in the area for a long time, you may already be familiar with the local inhabitants. However, if you're new to the area, you can ask other farmers or your local city office for advice. They will provide you with a list of the area's wildlife.

If you have observed that some of your hens and eggs have gone missing, but you're not sure who's to blame, here's a general guide:

- If your adult hens have gone missing and there has been no disturbance, a fox, dog, coyote, hawk, or owl is most likely to blame because only these predators can kill and remove an adult chicken from your coop.
- Snakes, rats, raccoons, and house cats are the most likely culprits if chicks go missing. When you notice feathers and wings far away from the site, you can be sure it's one of these predators.
- A weasel assault is most likely if you observe some of your chickens are damaged and dead but still on the premises. They are frequently more interested in your birds' internal organs.

- It's most likely a raccoon, hawk, or owl if your bird is dead and missing its head.
- Skunks, snakes, rats, raccoons, and possums are likely to eat the eggs.
- If your birds aren't dead but have bite marks, they may have been bitten by dogs, possums, weasels, or rodents.

When you detect these signs, the next step is to check if you can find any footprints on your property. After your investigation, it may be wise to set a trap to catch the culprit red-handed.

Installation of Security

If you can't protect your hens from predators and rodents, the objective of sheltering them is defeated. Use well-designed and entry-proof coops to safeguard your birds from these predators. Then encircle your property with a fence. These two options will keep ground predators out.

If you plan to use an electrified fence, ensure the voltage is low enough to stun the animals but not enough to kill them. It's also better to shock predators rather than kill them because a stunned animal will be less likely to return, whereas a dead one will be replaced immediately. You can also choose to have non-electrified fences installed.

Your fence needs to be buried to a depth of 2 to 4 feet, regardless of the fencing method, because certain predators will try to burrow their way to your birds. Then, whichever fence you choose, ensure it's sturdy enough to keep even the most powerful predator from entering. Something stronger, such as hardware mesh, is a much-used reinforcement to any coop setup.

5

HEALTHY CHICKEN PRODUCE HEALTHIER EGGS

Their diet directly influences chickens' productivity. They generally do not require a particular regiment of a primary feed. However, you may not be completely satisfied with the eggs they lay, whether the amount or size. As a result, you must carefully monitor their food to ensure that they get all the nutrients required to create and maintain egg production. The balance of three elements—vitamins, minerals, and proteins—is the foundation of a successful feed.

Calcium is necessary to develop eggs, so the bird must consume appropriate amounts or the eggshell will be transparent instead of the solid surface you want. Lack of nutrients can also result in a considerable reduction in egg production. To avoid this, add special feeds to their diet tailored explicitly for the types of birds.

Compound feed is a specifically formulated mixture fortified with vitamins, grain crops, and microelements to boost chicken egg production.

Regardless of why a farmer keeps chickens on their farm, the bird's health and productivity are always top priorities. To care for the hens' health, you must learn how to feed them, what kind of grain to add to their diet, and how often. You may receive eggs from laying chickens all year long if you correctly plan their diet.

WHAT CHICKENS EAT

Chickens eat various foods that help them stay healthy and capable of laying. I know you thought you were the only one that had to keep an eye on their diet!

Chickens are omnivores, meaning they eat everything. That implies they eat veggies, fruits, carbs, and proteins just like you. Apart from delectable clover, seeds, and other healthy items, they can be easily distracted by the number of bugs and critters they encounter when running throughout your yard.

Your hens instinctively know what they need to eat, but they like to try everything when searching for their next meal. It appears to be the only way they can figure out what's edible and what's not. As your females decide on their optimal dietary demands, lizards, toads, skinks, and even a tiny snake may be cast away.

As previously stated, fresh food and water are a daily requirement for all pets and livestock. The ideal feed for your chickens is layer feed. This feed type, which contains the proper balance of nutrients for laying hens, should be of good quality and purchased from a recognized supplier so that you can be sure there are no harmful additions included (Jacque Jacobs n.d).

Online vendors, hatcheries, shops, and farm supply outlets can help you find a suitable feed. Many providers may advise you on the best grain feeds to use, and they'll also sell the equipment you need to feed and water your hens. However, don't buy from a catalog unless you're sure the product is right for your flock.

Feed your chickens organically whenever possible. There are several trustworthy organic poultry feed vendors. It will be more expensive and more difficult to find everywhere.

Feeding becomes easier in the summer when your hens are more able to free range. Your flock will most likely prefer clover, Kentucky bluegrass, and buckwheat in addition to bugs and grain. However, additional dietary supplements are likely required during the colder months, as successful foraging will be limited (Jacque Jacobs n.d).

WATER MANAGEMENT

Like you, your hens will survive longer without food than they will without water. Your flock, of course, requires both to realize their full potential. Lack of consistent fresh water causes growth delays, early molting, stress, and changes in their egg-laying routines. Aside from automatic watering systems, which may be costly, a water mister can provide a fun location for your birds to drink while cooling off with the spray on hot summer days.

FEED MANAGEMENT

As previously said, your hens must eat and drink daily. Food is necessary for your hens' growth and development, but it also generates heat to keep their bodies warm and aids in producing nutritional eggs (Linden, 2015).

The food and water containers can be strategically organized to provide interest in the chicken run. When these containers are elevated above ground level, the birds will have more perching space and will be less likely to pollute them with their dung than when the containers are on the chicken run floor. Use your creativity to devise an approach to managing the containers so that the contents don't become soiled. The newest product people use or build themselves is a chicken picnic table. The chickens use the benches to perch on while eating at the tabletop.

Some chicken caretakers install feeders to an outer coop wall. Small openings on top will allow the chickens to obtain food and water without becoming contaminated by feces. The containers are simple to fill with grain and water without having to open the coop, which is convenient when the weather is bad.

CHICKEN FEED TYPES

Wheat

For chicken feeding, durum wheat is the best and most nutritious grain. Most chicken feed starts with wheat and then is bolstered by a range of other grains. Course scratch feeds or mashes should be used to bulk it up.

Oats

This grain can be added whole, rolled, or in a mash form. The amount of hull present determines the nutrient value of the oats.

Barley

As a whole grain, this is an excellent addition to scratch meals. It can also be rolled or crushed, and barley that has been soaked or boiled also works nicely.

Corn

Corn is a favorite of chickens. They will eat it whole, cracked, or crushed, on its own or combined with other grains.

Millet

Proso, often known as hog millet, is an excellent feed for growing and fattening. It is also good for laying chickens. It is frequently used as the second or third ingredient in many feeds.

Rye

Small amounts of rye can be added to scratch and mash diets, though it is not as tasty as the other grains.

Flax

This grain is excellent to add to scratch feed during molting, fall, and winter.

By-Products of Grain

Adding bran, shorts, and middling can benefit growing and laying rations. Fattening feeds include oat flour, feed, middling, and barley flour.

Fats

Most feeds contain a tiny amount of fat that serves as an energy source and aids in the absorption of crucial vitamins in the chicken's body. Excess fat is bad and can create severe intestinal issues in your hens.

Fats from animals and plants are high in energy. They help to increase mineral and vitamin absorption as well as aid in digestion. Adding a modest amount of fat to your chickens' diet may be helpful.

By-Products of Milk

All milk by-products aid in the fattening of laying hens and the production of high-quality eggs, and these ingredients are an essential addition to high-quality chicken feeds.

Fish Oil

Many different fish oil supplements are used in chick rations, winter feeds, and laying hen feeds, especially when their vegetable rations are scarce.

Balancers

Fillers and balancers are specifically produced food additives that chicken feed producers make to add to regular poultry feed as directed by the manufacturer (Manitoba, 1945).

SELECTING THE IDEAL FOOD FOR YOUR FLOCK

Goals for your chickens will determine the type of feed you choose for your backyard flock. Broilers and egg-laying chickens are treated differently, so make sure you know which type of birds you plan to raise before making dietary decisions for them.

Feeding Chicks

Chick feed is separated into two categories: starter feed (20 to 24 percent protein) and growth feed (18 percent protein). Starter feed is ideal for your new babies from hatching to roughly 6 weeks. When your chicks are 6 to 7 weeks old, switch them to growing mash, which is high in essential nutrients for their further growth and development.

Layers

Pullets just starting to lay should be fed organic, non-GMO (genetically modified organism) layer feed, which is high in critical nutrients and has around 16 percent protein. The pullets will eat this feed for the rest of their lives. There is an extensive range of suitable commercial feeds from which to choose.

Feeds for All Flocks

Most backyard chicken keepers' flocks contain hens of various ages. All Flock Feed is ideal for these birds' nutritional requirements. Most of these well-balanced diets include probiotics, which improve digestion and promote gut health. Adult birds will benefit from All Flock Feed as a maintenance feed.

Fermented Feed

Chickens benefit from the tasty nutrients released during fermentation when standard chicken feed is mixed with water and allowed to ferment naturally. Fermented feed is not only healthier for your chickens, but it is also less expensive in the long run.

Fermenting is a simple and quick process: Add a little water and a few drops of apple cider vinegar to whatever grain you usually give your chickens (¼ cup per chicken). Combine the ingredients in a nontoxic plastic container with 14 teaspoons of yeast, and mix thoroughly. Allow three to four days for the mixture to ferment, at which point it should smell like sourdough. The fermented feed is ready for your chickens to eat, and they will go crazy for it.

Pellets

This poultry feed is a low-wastage, sustainable adult chicken feed that has been converted into easy-to-store, transportable, and useful pellets.

Crumbles

Crumbles—crushed pellets ideal for chicks—are one size down from pellets.

Mash

For chickens to digest their food correctly, fresh water is as essential as any other feed. Mash is a coarsely crushed, varied, uncooked feed in powder form. The mash can be offered wet or dry and is suitable for both day-old chicks and adult birds.

Medicated Feed

Some chicken diets contain a coccidiostat, a prophylactic ingredient that helps kittens, puppies, cattle, and poultry have better intestinal health by slowing the growth and reproduction of the deadly parasitic Coccidian protozoa.

Unmedicated Feed

Unmedicated feed refers to all untreated chicken feed that does not contain a coccidiostat.

INGREDIENTS FOR FEEDING

Chickens require a diet rich in protein, fats, minerals, carbs, and vitamins for proper development. Does this ring a bell? The same necessary macro and micronutrients are required in your diet. Let's look at each of these nutritional components in further depth.

Macronutrients

Proteins, carbs, and fats are among the nutrients required for your backyard flock's optimal health, well-being, and productivity.

- Proteins

Proteins are essential energy sources and tools for constructing and repairing damaged tissues and cells, commonly known as the body's building blocks. Protein sources include meat, fish, milk, nuts, seeds, and bone meal. They are often the most expensive component of a poultry diet. The most acceptable choice for rearing a healthy chicken flock is well-balanced grain and protein feed.

- Carbs

Carbohydrates make up the majority of your hens' dietary requirements. They are necessary for healthy physiological function and energy. The starchy substances in the feed that assist in energy release make up these key components. Chickens cannot thrive on carbs alone, although they are essential in their diet.

- Fats

The essential rule for maintaining your healthy backyard flock is to keep fatty items out of their feed. As previously stated, chickens need minimal fat in their diet.

Micronutrients

The following micronutrients, which include vitamins, minerals, and riboflavin, are just as essential and critical for chicken health.

- Vitamin A

Vitamins A and other micronutrients are necessary for your flock's longevity. A vitamin A deficiency in your chickens can make them more susceptible to illnesses and colds. Increasing their consumption of greens, maize, and fish oil will add more to their diet.

- Vitamin D

Vitamin D insufficiency could cause limb weakness, bone abnormalities, and fragile eggshells in your flock. Increase the amount of fish oil in your chicken feed and encourage your flock to spend more time outside in the sun.

- Riboflavin

This vitamin, found in yeast, green feed, liver, and milk products, is necessary for chicks to grow and develop while in the shell and until they reach adulthood. A riboflavin deficit could cause curled toe paralysis in your flock.

- Minerals

Calcium, magnesium, phosphorus, potassium, and zinc are all essential minerals that play a role in bone strength and structure, tendon strength and flexibility, and eggshell production. These micronutrients are abundant in salt and certain green foods.

FEEDING YOUR FLOCK IN THE BEST WAYS

A well-balanced meal rich in vitamins, proteins, and minerals is essential for young chicks. One chick can usually be fed for six weeks with 2 pounds of dry starter mash. As your chicks grow, gradually increase the coarseness of the grains until the young pullets eat the same diet as the flock adults. A professionally made starter feed is frequently the most convenient option, although it can be somewhat costly. To avoid the feed clumping in the birds' mouths and generating undesired, potentially expensive digestive problems, use a flaky brand.

When starting with baby chicks, begin feeding them as soon as they are interested in eating. Several shallow containers or egg case flats of feed should be placed inside the brooder. Ensure that each chick masters the art of eating. Some grasp it immediately, while others take a little longer to realize they should be pecking at the food. If you observe a slow eater, you'll need to step in and help the weaker chick figure out how to eat.

According to Linden (2015), commercial feed contains many beneficial components. However, several crucial criteria will influence the sort of rations you choose, including the age of your flock, the breed, and whether your birds are laying hens or broilers.

Separate the little trays of fine grit from the feed in the brooder. Add a little broken wheat to the feed at 3 weeks, and at 4 weeks, whole wheat (Manitoba, 1945). A steady supply of milk will aid in calcium absorption by young chicks' delicate bones.

Make every effort to provide good-quality green grass to your flock for as long as possible. For newly hatched chicks, fall rye, oats, and alfalfa provide a nutritious spectrum. Crushed corn can be added to their diet to boost carbohydrate bulk.

If your location allows it, excellent healthy pasture feeding can help you save money on commercial feeds while also encouraging strong bone growth and glossy feather development.

Your chicks should be on a 50/50 mix of starter and developing mash by weeks 6 and 7. At 8 weeks, they can start on grower feed. They will eat this until they are 20 weeks old when they will begin laying. For the first week or so, do a mixed blend of the starter and grower feed so as not to upset any of their digestive systems. The chicks will also be introduced into the flock group, so ensure the feeders are at an appropriate height for both the younger and the older chickens. As you watch your babies integrate into the group, ensure they get enough of the feed, and that the older ones do not eat it all.

For egg-laying hens to be fully prolific and provide you with a quality product, they should be fed laying rations for the majority of the year, enhanced by additional protein supplements. Profit depends on consistent egg production, so it's critical to supplement your flock's diet with vitamins and minerals. To ensure your chickens produce the best eggs, increase their intake of alfalfa, clover, hay, coarse grains, and skim milk.

Your chickens may not drink enough milk or consume sufficient protein and minerals throughout the cold months. As a result, commercial fillers, balancers, laying concentrates, and various protein meal types must be added to their diet. Crushed oyster shells, limestone grit, and bone meal are all helpful additives for your flock.

SCRAPS FROM THE TABLE

Because table scraps aren't a regular part of your flock's diet, it's best to feed them in moderation. Chickens are known to be voracious eaters who will eat almost anything. Choose suitable scraps with care and start feeding them to your flock when they are between 3 and 4 months old. Chicks should not be fed scraps because they are still growing; instead, they should be encouraged to eat the growing mash (McMurray Staff, 2017).

✚ Suitable Scraps

The following scraps should be included in the chickens' diet (McMurray Staff, 2017):

- Only a tiny amount of mold-free bread
- Meats that have been cooked and chopped into little pieces
- Corn (raw, cooked, or dried)
- Berries, grapes, apples, watermelon, and other fruits
- Commercial cereals, rice, wheat, and other grains
- Peas, broccoli, shredded carrots, cabbage, spinach, potatoes, squash, lettuce, tomatoes, kale, yogurt, and pasta

━ Scraps to Avoid

The scraps that should be avoided, on the other hand, are:

- Sea salt
- Processed meats
- Uncooked meats
- Takeout foods and pastries
- Raw potato skins
- Pits and peels from avocados

- Soft drinks, coffee, and tea
- Dark chocolate
- Greasy foods
- Garlic
- Onions
- Red chilies
- Spoiled food

ORGANIC FEEDS

If you see eating organic as beneficial, you may want the same for your flock. Organic chicken feed will likely provide your backyard chickens with similar long-term health benefits. Organic foods are grown in a healthy, natural, and sustainable way, without pesticides or other harmful additives that may affect the finished product's quality and nutritional content. You might find two valuable organic goods: baby chick crumbs and mixed corn.

Some of the benefits of organic feed are as follows (Farm & Pet Place, 2016):

- There are no hazardous additives in the soil.
- Land management is well-maintained and sustainable.
- Natural water sources are not contaminated.
- There will be less environmental impact.

- There will be less harm to animals and wildlife.
- There are no contaminants or genetically modified foods produced.
- The feed is more nutritious.
- There are no genetically modified organisms (GMOs) in the food.
- There are few poisons in the soil and water.
- You're serving your family healthy, organic meat and eggs.

EMERGENCY FEED

In the craziness of life, you may have run out of chicken feed. To help move beyond feeling horrible about your lack of forethought, here are some quick, easy tips to soothe ruffled feathers and give yourself time to replace the chickens' feed (Arcuri, 2022):

- Hard-boiled eggs, cooled and chopped, make a delicious treat for your hungry brood.
- Good old table scraps will suffice for a day or two.
- Hand-plucked suitable grasses and clover will keep the flock happy.
- Porridge is an excellent standby in emergencies.

DELICIOUS SNACKS

Chickens look forward to special treats from time to time, like we all do. The only notable distinction is that their goodies should be healthy, not freshly baked cookies. Here are some fantastic treat ideas for your birds that will have them running to greet you. Mealworms are sure to be a massive hit with your flock. Adding blackberries, blueberries, grated carrots, and sunflower seeds to the mix will make it that much more delectable and nutritious.

Remember, no matter how much pleading, prodding, or cajoling your girls do, treats should be handed out with thoughtful consideration. You can provide these tempting morsels at certain times, such as before you leave for work in the morning or while teaching your flock to go into the coop at night.

If you stick to the 90/10 feeding rule, your hens will stay healthy and productive without acquiring excess weight. Ninety percent of their food should be their regular, nutritional sustenance, while 10 percent can be treats.

AVOIDING FEEDING MISTAKES

According to Linden (2015), the most difficult problem is determining the best nutrition for your chickens to keep them in optimum health. As a result, there may be insufficient egg production and birds may succumb to disease quickly. You could be depriving your flock of essential nutrients if you aren't aware of these potentially dangerous mistakes.

A miscalculation of calcium levels in layer feed may be too high for young birds. Mixing scratch grains like broken corn with commercial feeds depletes the feed's protein, vitamin, and mineral content.

Another issue is not giving your chickens enough of the proper diet. The more adequately fed your hens are, the more likely they will live a long and healthy life. This is an investment because feed accounts for more than 70 percent of the cost of rearing your flock.

YOUR CHICKENS' WATER REQUIREMENTS

We rarely consider the importance of water in the coop, even though it is essential for productivity and survival because it is routine and the most straightforward task for our flock. Fill the water during the morning and afternoon checks and keep it cool in the summer and not frozen in the winter.

Water is necessary for your chickens for a variety of reasons. The first benefit is that it aids with temperature regulation. Chickens don't have sweat glands but shed heat only through their feet, combs, wattles, panting, and by expanding their wings. Those small areas to release heat can't compete with the abundance of feathers all over their body. Their body temperature is slightly higher than ours. When the temperature is over 100°F, water intake will assist in managing their temperature, and other avenues must also be taken to cool them, such as a fan, shade, and cold treats.

Chicken keepers supply their hens with electrolyte water to reduce the potential harm to their chickens from the heat. Laying can halt or cease if they do not drink enough water. Dehydration prevents their bodies from functioning normally and can quickly cause lethargy and even death in the summer.

The presence of water assists in a hen's digestion. It breaks down the food into an easily digestible state. The nutrients are moved through the body via blood (which contains a lot of water) and given to the cells. Digestion problems, such as sour crops, might occur if there isn't enough water.

Finally, their brain health needs to be considered. A dehydrated brain has cluttered, confused, and unclear thoughts, causing them to be significantly more vulnerable to predation or injury.

Adult Hens

A general estimate is that each hen should drink around 2 cups of water every day. Consider the following scenario: A flock of six chickens needs approximately 12 cups of water per day, and you can do the rest of the math for more chickens, right?

Checking the water stations at least twice a day when you gather your eggs should be sufficient. However, the precise figure will be determined by a few different factors. When it's hot outside, your hens will drink more. The size of the bird, whether it is free range, and whether it is an egg layer are all factors that can influence how much water they drink. Free-range hens may drink a little less since they acquire moisture from other sources. Egg layers will consume more than those who do not lay eggs.

Chicks

Once your chicks have been exposed to the water source, they will remember where it is and return to it whenever they need to drink. Don't confuse them by moving the waterers around. You should keep the water in one location so they don't have to look for it. Your babies should be lively, conversational, and bright-eyed, getting hydrated regularly on their own.

Waterer Quantity and Quality

On average, you should provide one waterer for every six to eight chickens. Place one or two waterers if you have a separate run from the coop. If you have a hen who thinks the waterers are her personal property and refuses to share, keeping them a decent distance apart is always a good idea. Similarly, if you allow your flock to roam freely, you must have a few waterers on the range.

Wherever you put the water, make sure it's high enough to avoid dust, straw, and poop from being scratched into the water. Waterers should always be placed in shady areas to keep the water from being too hot to consume or evaporating in the heat. If you have bantams, you may need to build a ramp up to the waterer with bricks or stairs.

Keeping Your Waterer Clean

In an ideal world, your waterers should be rinsed and refilled daily. However, this isn't always possible because most of us have hectic schedules. Just make sure it happens regularly. Then, once a month, give your waterers a thorough cleaning. Scrubbing and rinsing with fresh water, vinegar, or a bleach solution is quick and easy. You can feel the slick and slimy biofilm on the sides of the container. You will get biofilm if you do not clean the water frequently enough.

Keep your waterers out of direct sunlight to avoid organisms increasing due to the light and heat. If you utilize range waterers, attempt to keep wild birds away from the waterer itself, especially now that avian influenza is a concern.

It's critical to double-check your equipment's functionality at least once a week. Waterers freeze quickly in cold areas; therefore, you may need to change the water more than once a day.

It's unusual for a healthy chicken to refuse to drink. However, there are a few circumstances to keep an eye on:

- Is there an alpha hen defending the water source in your yard? If the answer is yes, providing a second waterer is a straightforward solution. Make sure it's far enough away from the first waterer so the alpha hen can't protect both simultaneously.
- If your hen refuses to drink and appears sick, you'll need to spend one-on-one time with her to observe and apply the treatment. Giving her

water by syringe may be necessary to get her hydrated again. The water must be lukewarm and you need to push the water in slowly, so she does not choke.

- Dehydration is more common in the summer, but it can happen at any time of the year. Excessive heat and humidity can cause a hen to become sick quickly.
- Panting, opening her beak, and holding her wings away from her body are the first symptoms of discomfort. These indicators communicate that she is feeling overheated and uncomfortable. She may also have a pale comb and wattle. You should act quickly before the situation worsens.
- Even though it may sound unusual, hens can suffer from diarrhea because they drink more water yet eat less, causing their excrement to be watery. She is now in risky terrain and requires quick treatment if she becomes lethargic or lame.

A Dehydration Treatment

If your chicken becomes dehydrated due to the heat and humidity, you should remove them from the sun and heat as soon as possible. Use a children's electrolyte solution to rehydrate them as quickly as possible. If you don't have any on hand, you can prepare your own electrolyte solution with 2 teaspoons of granulated sugar, 14 teaspoons of sea salt, and 14 teaspoons of baking soda. This mixture should be combined with 2 cups of water and stirred until completely dissolved.

6

PROTECT PRODUCT

Collecting eggs is the most exciting part of being a newbie backyard chicken keeper. You'll need a basic understanding of egg production and collection and what it takes to improve egg quality and quantity. Without further ado, let's get down to business and learn how backyard hens can give you the most extraordinary eggs you've ever tasted!

WHAT TO ANTICIPATE

Each hen can lay one egg daily, albeit not every hen will do so. With this in mind, you must be aware of your chickens' behavior.

Your ladies are unlikely to lay simultaneously, so laying will take place throughout the day, depending on each hen's laying cycle. The laying cycle is controlled by the hen's exposure to light (Jacob, n.d.-b). Her very first egg is usually laid early in the morning. The next will appear roughly twenty-six hours later, the length of time it takes for an egg to form in the hen's reproductive system. Check that coop in the morning and at night to grab those eggs.

On an egg production graph, you'll observe that production peaks from 20 to 75 weeks and then gradually declines. Some backyard chickens can produce eggs for up to four years, with the number of eggs decreasing somewhat each year. Egg output will decrease with age; however, the rate at which this process occurs is determined by the following criteria:

Breed

Some birds have been bred to lay more eggs than others. Leghorns lay an average of 250–300, Rhode Island Reds produce around 250 eggs, and a Golden Comet will produce an average of 280 eggs in a good year.

Pullet Management

There's no reason why your chickens shouldn't provide you with plenty of eggs if they've had a healthy start, well-balanced meals, plenty of fresh water, enough area to free range, and a spacious, safe coop. The health of your pullets directly correlates to egg-laying production.

Light Exposure

As previously said, light encourages your hens to lay. Light stimulation has boosted egg production in hens known as "long-season breeders." If your flock has lived a healthy outdoor life and has been exposed to laying lights after dark, these hens will most likely lay more eggs than other birds who have not been exposed to the additional lighting.

Nutrition and a Healthy Diet

Layers fed a well-balanced diet of suitable feed should be successful. Laying hens will produce higher-quality eggs if they consume a calcium-rich diet.

Space

For laying hens to produce well, they require adequate space. Please stick to the square-foot-per-chicken rules mentioned earlier. An overcrowded hen is a stressed hen and, therefore, that can affect its production. Hens with plenty of perching room and nesting boxes will lay more eggs consistently.

HOW TO IDENTIFY LAYING HENS

The deeper your grasp of the breed, the more you will be to recognize when the birds are ready to lay.

The red comb and wattles of some types of laying hens become more vibrant. In other breeds, the coloring becomes pale on the vent, beak, face, and legs with yellow pigments, such as Rhode Island Reds.

Another way is to assess the hen's abdomen area's growing size. The fuller the hen's abdomen, the more likely she is about to lay an egg.

A broody hen is a sign that she may be about to lay, but not always. They'll scratch and fuss in the nesting box or locate another place to lay their eggs. It is often thought a predator had taken a hen until they returned with a dozen chicks, bringing relief to the chicken keeper.

INTERNAL FACTORS THAT AFFECT EGG LAYING

A pullet will begin her laying cycle between 18 and 20 weeks. A pullet's first eggs will be smaller than a hen who has been laying for a while. It may also be malformed or otherwise defective. In a young bird, this is okay because it takes time to get the machinery working correctly, like making that first pancake. The first one to two years of production are the most prolific, and after that, the number of eggs produced gradually decreases with time. Hens that don't start laying until they're 7 or 8 years old are rare.

The breed determines the length of time your hen lays. Many of the production chickens are exhausted after only three years. The flock will be culled and replaced with new birds in commercial farming. Heritage breeds will lay for extended periods, though not in the same quantities as production hens.

Let's look at how the internal elements can influence a hen's egg production:

Molting

In the first year, the pullets will not molt. They will molt in their second winter after completing their first laying cycle, which will take fifteen to eighteen months. It is stated that the best layers molt earlier and faster to return to production. There's nothing you can do to stop the molting process. You can, however, provide good quality feed with higher protein content, at around 18 percent. Once a week, give them vitamins and electrolytes in their water and make sure they get enough calcium.

Parasites

Intestinal worms, lice, and mites are examples of parasites that may affect your girls' laying. A daily health check of your hens can prevent parasites from quickly increasing because they can deplete a hen's nourishment and cause anemia. A bath may be needed if they are not taking a dust bath themselves to keep the parasites at bay.

Disease

Several infectious diseases can cause a reduction in egg production. Infections, such as avian coryza, or the common cold, will go away on their own. Fowl pox, coccidiosis, infectious bronchitis, and avian influenza necessitate a more vigorous approach. Your veterinarian may prescribe antibiotics, but flock owners usually pick up antibiotics from a farm store to treat their animals. If the remedies performed are not making an improvement, seeking help from a professional is necessary. If you notice a chicken may be ill, please segregate them immediately. It will lessen the chance of the disease spreading and give you time to figure out what you are dealing with and treat her.

EXTERNAL FACTORS THAT AFFECT EGG LAYING

Not only can internal variables influence egg-laying, but so can external influences.

Water and Food

Food and water are the easiest to monitor because you provide them. When hens start laying, proper nutrition consists of a high-protein, high-quality meal with 16 percent protein. Some chicken keepers try to save money by mixing their own feed, which is good if you're a chicken nutritionist, but most people don't do it correctly. Feed manufacturers invest millions of dollars in research, and the feed is adequately combined with the right quantities of additives. Unless you have a large flock, making your feed isn't cost-effective when compared to a 50-pound bag at 12 to 15 dollars.

A hen must have constant access to cool, clean water to lay consistently. Your job is to ensure she will drink often by placing it in a shaded area to keep it cool as well as ensuring it is elevated to keep the dirt out. In the winter, the challenge is to keep it from freezing. If you have electricity to the run or coop, you can purchase and use an electric dog water bowl.

With feed, it's the same thing. If laying hens aren't fed properly, it will affect the quantity and quality of their eggs. A hen should gradually be moved from starter to layer feed, which contains 16 percent protein, at the age of 18 to 20 weeks. You can use 16 percent protein formulas till the chicks reach laying age if you have a flock of diverse ages.

Calcium

Hens also require extra calcium that should be accessible daily. This excess calcium aids in the maintenance of their bones and the production of solid eggshells. The hens' bodies will leach calcium from their bones to make eggshells, making them brittle. Eggshells will become as thin as parchment or non-existent if calcium is absent.

Poisoning

Moldy or contaminated feed is one of the most common causes of poisoning. Mold spores grow when the material becomes damp, producing the mycotoxins that poison the hen. Poisoning occurs infrequently in backyard flocks and is usually unintentional. Musty bedding is another source of mycotoxin, so hay/straw bales should be stored outside the coop during the winter.

Botulism is another relatively common poison. Chickens may peck at a dead mouse or similar carcass and swallow the neurotoxin produced by bacteria. Allowing the birds to eat little corpses in the compost heap is not a good idea.

Nesting Boxes

Have you provided your hens with enough nesting boxes? For every three hens, one nesting box should be provided. You can often find a few ladies sharing the same one even when other boxes are available. If they are not pecking at each other, you can leave them. If you don't have enough boxes, they'll find another location to lay their eggs, so you'll be looking for impromptu nests wherever they're allowed to roam. A heavy breed hen's nesting box should be around 14 inches square with nest material like straw or shredded newspaper. Place a cardboard square under the nesting material to prevent eggs from breaking. Toss it out and replace it as it becomes soiled.

EGG LAYING DROPS SUDDENLY

If you're used to collecting a dozen or more daily and suddenly find yourself with only five or six, you'll have to do some investigative work.

Predators

Is there anyone in your flock who eats eggs? A hen will occasionally break an egg in the nest and consume it. As the hen lays the egg, it will softly roll away from her, making it unavailable for consumption. Collecting eggs regularly or using nest boxes with a roll-away method can remedy this. If you have a predator problem, like snakes or rodents taking eggs, ensure there isn't any way for them to get into the coop.

Hidden Eggs

Do you keep your chickens in a pasture? If that's the case, you might have a couple of eggs stashed in the tall grass. Occasionally a hen vanishes to return with chicks after some time. Search behind plants and shrubs and in little darkened spaces where she might be hiding them.

Daylight

To complete the egg development and laying process, hens require fourteen to sixteen hours of daylight. As the days become shorter and the seasons change, you'll notice a drop in the number of eggs laid. This natural slowing down is perfect because it allows your hen's body to rest throughout the winter. Read our section on controlled lighting below if you still want your hens to lay during this time.

Stress or Changes in Their Routine

Hens are creatures of habit, so any change to their schedule will most certainly cause them to stop laying for a season. It could be as small as moving a feeder or waterer around that disturbs one or two fearful flock members. More significant changes, such as relocating them all to a new place, will likely generate considerable anxiety. Don't worry; they'll return to work once the dust has settled and a new routine is in place.

STILL NOT LAYING?

Many people successfully cross-breed backyard stock; however, this sometimes produces oddities. You may occasionally encounter a hen unable to lay eggs due to birth abnormalities or congenital problems. You'll often be dealing with hens who have a prolapsed vent or egg yolk peritonitis.

Controlled Lighting

The daylight a hen receives controls her internal system for laying eggs; she needs at least fourteen hours of light to continue laying. The summer months provide enough light to sustain laying, but what happens when the hours of daylight decrease? The hen is preparing to molt during this time. She will lose the majority of her feathers during the molting process and replace them with new feathers. Laying ceases now because feathers contain around 85 percent protein, and producing new feathers is nutritionally intensive. The molting process takes an average of seven to eight weeks. Please stick to your daily health checks now because they are more susceptible to getting sick.

The average daylight in the United States during winter is only nine and a half hours. This decrease in sunlight allows the hens to sleep. The flock must have some time to rest. Continuous laying, according to some long-time chicken caretakers and vets, can cause the vent to prolapse or ovarian cancer. In the long run, it is better to allow chickens to recoup throughout the winter.

If you decide that you want them to lay through the winter, you must provide your hens with artificial lighting in the coop. A 40w light bulb (make sure it's not a fluorescent bulb) will suffice. Please ensure the light source is out of reach of the chickens and away from dry bedding or other potentially flammable materials when installing it. Ensure the light bulb is securely attached; use a backup fitting if the first fails and the light falls to the floor. Use wire or chain metal for the fixing because pests like rats can chew through a string.

You can use a timer to set the light to come on from 4 a.m. to 8 a.m. Artificial light should be added in the morning rather than the evening to avoid stressing the birds. During the winter, you'll need to time your fake light timer to match the sunset time to keep your hens' daylight consistent at around fourteen hours. As the winter progresses, you will need to leave your light bulb on for more extended periods to maintain the fourteen-hour rule. As March approaches and natural daylight lengthens, you'll want to reduce the time you use the light.

WHEN AND HOW OFTEN TO COLLECT EGGS

Make sure that the eggs you harvest are as clean as possible. Check each one as you pick it up. If there is a little dirt on one, use a dry cloth to wipe it. This helps you limit the amount of egg cleaning required afterward and unnecessarily get the others in the basket dirty.

Always gather eggs as early and as often as possible. Collecting twice a day is part of a keeper's regular schedule. Leaving eggs in the nesting boxes overnight will entice your chickens to create a habit of eating the eggs. One of the reasons chickens begin eating raw eggs is egg breakage. If you leave eggs overnight, your chickens may accidentally step on them or knock them onto the coop floor while moving around at night.

When retrieving your eggs, earlier is always better. Most hens do not lay eggs past 10 in the morning. This way, your flock has less time for mishaps and developing a taste for eggs. Do not go more than a day without gathering eggs.

CLEANING, STORING, AND REFRIGERATING EGGS

There is a high possibility that you will find eggs with poop on them when gathering them. If you find excrement in the nesting boxes when collecting eggs, clean it up very well and replenish the straw or shavings. If too much waste accumulates on an egg, it might become inedible and possibly hazardous. Cleaning your eggs properly will save you and your family from becoming sick.

You can use two methods to clean chicken eggs: dry or wet. Dry cleaning is better than wet cleaning because it does not wash off the egg's bloom (the antibacterial protective covering). To dry clean, wipe the eggs with an abrasive sponge or loofah. Some folks even use fine sandpaper. No matter what you choose, these solutions remove all dirt and feces from the shell.

Wet washing may still be required when the eggs are dirty or have egg yolk stuck to the shells. Always wash your eggs under warm running water from a tap. Ensure the water is warmer than the egg's temperature, but make sure the water is not too hot. After wet cleaning, use a paper towel to dry the eggs, then set them in a clean, open carton, an egg basket, or on a wire rack. Then you can sanitize the cleaned eggs by spraying them with a solution of bleach diluted with water.

If you are storing your eggs in the fridge, they can last for a month from the gathering day. Labeling your egg cartons will help you calculate when your eggs will go bad, sparing you from eating rotten eggs. If you wet clean your eggs, they must be refrigerated because you have rinsed off the bloom. If you dry clean the eggs, you can leave them unrefrigerated for up to a month. However, note that they will start to lose their exquisite taste after two weeks. After this time, it is recommended to use freshly-laid eggs for baking or hard-boiling, so you will not notice the reduced taste quality. Always wet wash your dry-cleaned eggs before usage.

If you forget to identify your egg or cannot recall how long your eggs have been in your kitchen, it is easy to evaluate their freshness using the float test. For the float test, place the eggs in a water-filled bowl. An egg floats when it has evaporated too much within, leading it to have a huge air pocket. If the egg floats, it is spoiled. If it sinks, it is okay.

You can also candle your egg to check if it is still fresh. When you candle an egg, you hold a light near the egg to help you see the inside. Only a bright light and a dark room are needed. Candle an egg by holding an intense light against the eggshell to view the air sac size inside. If the air sacs in the egg are large, they are not fresh. If they are little, they are fresh.

If you wish to raise your own chicks, you must candle your eggs to verify that they are fertilized and thriving. You can utilize the bright light and dark room system here also. To achieve this, carefully hold the egg up to the light. Hold the bigger end of the egg against the light, then spin the egg slowly to observe the embryo inside. Do this as quickly as possible because the light may make the embryo too hot. You must also be sure not to remove the eggs from the incubator for more than twenty to thirty minutes. If you want more efficient and exact handling, visit your local poultry or farm supply store for an egg-candling apparatus. As a newbie to backyard chicken keeping, waiting until you have more experience before trying to incubate your eggs to produce chicks is suggested.

7

THE CHICKEN CLUB

There is no such thing as democracy or equality in a flock. Chickens preserve social order through authoritarian rule. Their social organization is dubbed the pecking order since they literally peck one another into submission.

The pecking order has several complexities. Sub-hierarchies confound societal rules, but chickens usually live in peace. In a mixed flock, there are three sub-hierarchies: hen-to-hen, rooster-to-hen, and rooster-to-rooster.

The alpha hen rules the flock. Her rank gives her access to the coop and yard's best sections. Her subordinates always yield so she can get the best nest, dust bath, shaded napping area, preferred roosting spot, and anything else she deems is hers. The beta gets the second choice, and so on. If a lower-ranking hen doesn't surrender or is hesitant to move, she may get an angry look. The subordinate may get a head peck, chest bump, or other demonstration of dominance.

The queen's role isn't all privilege. Her wings carry the flock's well-being and peace. As a strong leader, she must preserve flock order. The queen warns of danger and guides the others to safety. A good queen can eat first, but she rarely does. While guarding the flock, she lets the others eat. The queen eats when they're done eating or when her beta is available to stand watch.

Higher-ranking chickens often serve as judges, mediators, and peacekeepers. Their tasks vary with flock size and dynamics. The queen or another high-ranking hen will intervene if a flock fight lasts too long. The mediator-judge will peck the troublemakers. She may jump-kick and flog the one she deems more responsible. As you can expect, this chicken was not high on the pecking order. High-ranking chickens or the queen patrol the dining area throughout meals, like lunch ladies, to keep the peace. The queen waits for each flock member to return home at dusk as if taking attendance. She might harass younger birds she doesn't consider to be flock members and block their entry.

Roosters are usually alpha or flock rulers. He protects, feeds, and ensures the flock's unity, like a flock queen with all the privileges but less duty. If there's more than one rooster, they'll rank themselves and assign rights and rules separate from their flock rating.

CHICKEN CALLS

Research has discovered that hens can generate at least twenty-four distinct noises. The sounds combined with actions, such as a head tilt, a gaze, a wing flap, or a dash, can communicate various things, such as "Hawk! Defcon 2!" "Squirrel alert!" or "Hey, I found a lizard!"

With recording technology and artificial intelligence software, researchers have been able to anticipate and determine whether hens are pleased, stressed, or ill based on the sounds, tone, and volume of their vocalizations. You and I won't have AI to assist us in translating chicken speak, but with enough listening and observation, you can still learn what your chickens are attempting to communicate.

Baby Talk

The charming, cheerful sounds we associate with chicks are sounds of contentment. When they're happy during nap or cuddling time, they will make a chicken purr.

Their noises of dissatisfaction are intense and loud. You'll hear the surprising sound when you accidentally sneak up on them. They vocalize a cry signifying dread when you reach into the brooder to pick them up before they've gotten acquainted with you. They produce sounds of anguish when they're too hot, too cold, or hungry. When lost or if they can't see their companions, they make a loud, frantic call to their mates.

Mama Calls

Mama hens will have distinct calls and sounds when telling their chicks to follow closely when they've located some food, warning the chicks of potential hazards, and instructing them to keep concealed. Mama hens will even cluck and speak with their chicks when inside the eggs—and the chicks chirp back!

Angry Birds

You'll undoubtedly face her fury if you interrupt a hen while she's laying or broody. When a hen "goes broody," her hormones signal that she must sit on and hatch some eggs. Disturbing a laying or broody hen will result in an outraged scream of "GO AWAY!" and some more colorful cackles. The hen may also hiss, growl, and puff herself out to look more threatening.

At other times, birds may growl, complain, and grumble at night when they don't want another hen roosting too close to them. They'll peck the other hens while asking them to scram. The pecked hens will vocalize fear and virtually cry, "Ouch!" When you handle a hen who doesn't want to be picked up, she'll sure squawk something like, "Let me go! Help!"

Chick Chat

The flock will communicate throughout the day, as when they're following one another to a great feeding or dusting site, saying, "This is a good spot!" or "Let's go this way." Sometimes they merely sound like they're catching up on the latest gossip.

When going into the yard, chickens may approach you and cluck various greetings. If they become enthusiastic or think you have treats, some will fly from wherever they may be while making loud cackles, as if to say, "Hey! Wait for me! I'm coming!" They are informing the others of what is happening and letting you know they are coming, just like any other pet would do.

COMMON CAUSES OF BULLYING

Now, let's take a closer look at a few of the most typical causes of Bullying (*Chicken bullying: How to stop them pecking each other*, 2021).

Stress

Chickens are creatures of habit, and anything that disrupts their routine might cause them to become stressed. The introduction of new flock members, the loss of a flock mate, the change of feed, the introduction of new accommodations, and a variety of other minor issues are all significant pressures.

Usually, they respond to nervousness by going off laying for a few days and becoming quieter than usual. Still, in rare cases, tension may force one hen to act out of character and become violent toward a flock mate. Additionally, the threat of a predator or a ferocious farm dog lurking nearby could cause anxiety.

Boredom

Boredom aggressiveness is particularly prevalent during the winter months. Because they are unable or reluctant to go outside due to the cold and have nothing else to do, they begin plucking feathers. It would be great if it remained a minor issue with only irregular picking, but it has the potential to escalate into a problem of picking by a bunch of hens.

Sickness

It is instinctive for chickens to recognize when one of their own is ill. In the wild, chickens will often remove a sick or ill chick from the flock if she poses a threat to the other chickens.

Overcrowding

The most common cause of bullying is overcrowding. Many chicken caretakers make the mistake of buying or hatching chicks as a spur-of-the-moment decision, assuming that one or two more won't hurt. It works in the summer because they are not in the coop as much but is more difficult in the winter when they are inside. Remember that each large bird needs 5 square feet in the enclosure and 15 square feet in the run. It is probable that, if there are limited spaces, mischief will occur.

Contemplate what it would be like to spend the entire winter with your family in one room. Nerves will fray and temper tantrums will erupt from time to time, regardless of how much you love your family. Here's when you can learn more about how much space hens need.

HOW CAN WE PREVENT BULLYING?

Now that we've discovered the most common causes of bullying, let's look at how to prevent it.

Recognize the Nature of the Problem

If you don't have a rooster, your flock will form a pecking order, with a few hens taking command when the roosters aren't around. Look for these commanding hens and keep an eye on them as they seize control of the flock. They may peck at other hens in certain circumstances, which is somewhat natural. Pay attention to pecking and look for chickens that are losing feathers or bleeding. These chickens are in danger, and you must act quickly to protect them and put an end to the problem.

Separate the injured chicken, address the wounded skin, and allow them to rest. A watchful eye will be necessary when releasing her back into the flock until the two can get reacquainted without coming into physical contact. If hens are fighting they should be separated. This isn't always needed, but it does help to lessen the likelihood of aggression while still allowing for some socialization (Coop, 2021).

Reset the flock's pecking order

Removing the flock's unfriendly chickens will help restore order. After the problem hens have been removed from the flock, the remaining hens will strive to form a new order under the leadership of new lead hens. Reintroduce the aggressive chickens after a week so they can make their way back into the group. If the hens continue to be a nuisance, you should confine them to an isolation enclosure near your regular run. They will be able to see the other hens but cannot act aggressively toward them. As a result, they will soon lose their will to attack and fight the other chickens.

Bring a Rooster Into the House

When a rooster isn't around, hens become more aggressive than usual. When you introduce a rooster to the flock, he will keep the hens from getting violent by controlling the hierarchical structure. You might want to buy more than one rooster, depending on the size of your flock. Generally, you should keep one rooster for every ten hens in your flock. Although the rooster will assist in reducing hen fights, he may pose a threat of aggression to humans and other animals in your home. Ensure you follow all local rules before introducing a rooster to your flock. City and county ordinances may limit or prohibit the number of roosters maintained in your area.

CONCLUSION

We've made it to the end of the book, and I want to thank you for sticking with me. You did an excellent job! I hope you have gained a wealth of knowledge from these chapters, and I am confident you will succeed in your chicken-raising endeavor.

I hope that this book has given you a good foundation for what you should think about before raising chickens. This book was written for starters and includes a guide to breeds, information on the housing and facilities they require, feed facts, how to maintain their health, and egg production. It should be regarded as a one-stop shop for everything a newcomer to chickens needs to know.

After reading the book, you should understand the advantages of chickens, the factors to consider before beginning the journey of raising chickens, and how to choose the right breed for your needs. You'll know where to get chickens and the perfect number to start with for your backyard.

You'll understand the various chicken housing and run options and whether you should buy or build a coop. Carefully consider shelter for your chickens in terms of size, location, insulation, and ventilation.

Chickens are wonderful companions. They make lovely pets and, more importantly, provide us with delicious eggs. Chickens are popular among most people, and only space and local ordinances prevent people from keeping them. Taking care of your chickens will just take a few minutes of your time each day.

The keeping of animals is heavily regulated in most urban areas. You must first determine whether your local community allows chickens and what boundaries, if necessary, you must raise the chickens within. You might want to see if there are any rules about coop size and design, minimum distances between the coop and the houses, and so on. Roosters are not permitted in most cities because they are noisy and may cause disturbance to your neighbors. The majority of people do not want to be awakened at 5 a.m. It's also a good idea to let your neighbors know about your backyard chicken plans so you can address any concerns they may have. Assure them that you'll only have hens and keep the coop clean to avoid any unpleasant odors. If you don't, you might face injunctions after you've already started working on your project. You won't have to worry about it if you live in an agricultural zone, have a lot of land, or are far away from neighbors.

Chickens are rarely sick if they are properly raised. In most cases, chicks are vaccinated against all the common diseases at the hatchery. You will be responsible for keeping them healthy by properly feeding them, cleaning their coops, and protecting them from predators. Allow them to free range in the sunlight, forage, and search for snacks in the grass. Provide a sandy area where they can bathe to protect them from pests. Do a daily health check on your flock as you collect eggs. As soon as you notice a sick chicken, separate it from the rest of the flock so you can figure out what it's sick from, apply first aid, and determine whether it's contagious.

When it comes to raising a pet, the noble yet mighty chicken may be a good option for you to consider, whether you want a low-maintenance pet or one that will provide your family with fresh eggs. Why would you waste your time and money on any other kind of pet when there are so many fun-loving, gorgeous breeds?

Now is the time to act on that dream and start your plan to provide a good home for these fantastic creatures. I hope you had a great time, and it has been a rewarding learning experience for you and your family.

Congratulations once again for getting one step closer to raising backyard chickens. I'm sure it'll bring you many pleasures and memories in the future.

PLEASE LEAVE A REVIEW

What if someone was in your shoes who didn't have the answers that you have after reading the book? You know their challenges and that they are looking for answers, but they don't know where to look. Leave a review for the book to help them get the answers you have now. It doesn't cost you a thing, but a little bit of your time. Give them your expertise and honest review so they can be in your shoes.

Please leave a review here by scanning the QR code:

Many thanks for considering my request.

REFERENCES

"Pros and Cons of Backyard Chickens." *Once a Month Meals*, 23 Sept. 2012, onceamonthmeals.com/blog/series/get-real/pros-and-cons-of-backyard-chickens

Teen Sports and Mental Health: 10 Mental Benefits of Sports. (2021, December 8). Newport Academy. https://www.newportacademy.com/resources/mental-health/sports-and-mental-health/

.Arcuri, L. (2022, March 3). *What to feed chickens or laying hens*. The Spruce. https://www.thespruce.com/feeding-your-chickens-or-laying-hens-3016556

Caughey, M. (2012, July 5). *Caring for your flock on a daily, weekly, monthly and seasonal basis*. Tilly's Nest. https://www.tillysnest.com/2012/07/caring-for-your-flock-on-daily-weekly-html/

Chicken bullying: How to stop them pecking each other. (2021, May 12). The Happy Chicken Coop. https://www.thehappychickencoop.com/chicken-bullying/

Freeman, P. (2022, March 31). *Buying a carton of eggs? Get the labeling facts first*. Backyard Poultry. https://backyardpoultry.iamcountryside.com/eggs-meat/egg-carton-labels-misleading/

Jacob, J. (n.d.-a). *Normal behaviors of chickens in small and backyard poultry flocks*. Poultry Extension. https://poultry.extension.org/articles/poultry-behavior/normal-behaviors-of-chickens-in-small-and-backyard-poultry-flocks/

Jacob, J. (n.d.-b). *Raising chickens for egg production*. Poultry Extension. https://poultry.extension.org/articles/poultry-management/raising-chickens-for-egg-production/

Johnson, R. (2018, May 24). *The importance of lighting in poultry production*. The Poultry Site. https://www.thepoultrysite.com/articles/the-importance-of-lighting-in-poultry-production

Linden, J. (2015, February). *Nutrition for the backyard flock*. The Poultry

Site. https://www.thepoultrysite.com/articles/nutrition-for-the-backyard-flock

Lofgren, E. (2014). *The backyard chicken bible: The complete guide to raising chickens.* Betterway Home.

McMurray Staff. (2017, May 11). *Safe table scraps for chickens.* Murray McMurray Hatchery. https://blog.mcmurrayhatchery.com/2017/05/11/safe-table-scraps-chickens/

Ridgerunner. (2015, January 24). *How much room do chickens need?* Backyard Chickens. https://www.backyardchickens.com/articles/how-much-room-do-chickens-need.66180/

Shea Mormino, K. (2012, April 5). *Droppings boards, because poop happens.* The Chicken Chick. https://the-chicken-chick.com/droppings-boards-because-poop-happens/

Smith, K. (2020a, June 26). *Top 20 chicken breeds for your backyard coop.* Backyard Chicken Coops. https://www.backyardchickencoops.com.au/blogs/learning-centre/top-20-chicken-breeds-for-your-backyard-coop

Smith, K. (2020b, July 16). *When will my chickens start laying eggs?* Backyard Chicken Coops. https://www.backyardchickencoops.com.au/blogs/learning-centre/when-will-my-chickens-start-laying-eggs

Coop, The Happy Chicken. "Chicken Bullying: How to Stop Them Pecking Each Other." *The Happy Chicken Coop*, 9 June 2022, www.thehappychickencoop.com/chicken-bullying.

Organic Chicken Feed – A Complete Guide. (2019, May 3). Farm & Pet Place. https://www.farmandpetplace.co.uk/organic-chicken-feed-a-complete-guide/

Agriculture | Province of Manitoba. (1945, June). Province of Manitoba - Agriculture. https://www.gov.mb.ca/agriculture/livestock/production/poultry/poultry-rations-and-feeding-methods.html

Jacque Jacobs, D. (n.d.). *FEEDING CHICKENS FOR EGG PRODUCTION IN SMALL AND BACKYARD FLOCKS – Small and backyard poultry.* SMALL AND BACKYARD POULTRY. https://poultry.extension.org/articles/feeds-and-feeding-of-poultry/feeding-chickens-for-egg-production/

Made in the USA
Monee, IL
29 November 2024

71636679R00096